The *Song* of the Ages

Part I: The Summit of Truth

NICK PADOVANI

E xulon
LITE

www.xulonpress.com

Table of Contents

Acknowledgements

Friendship is such a wonderful avenue by which the love of God is manifested. I am thankful for the dear friends around me, particularly those who helped edit this book, and the many more who encouraged its completion.

A special thank you to Roland, not only for his insightful eye, but for being a spiritual father to myself and many others.

And thank you to Jeff, a true and lasting friend.

And to Dylan. Thank you for the glory you embody.

My wife is an ever-present spring from which the love and mercy of God flows. You are my greatest encourager.
Thank you Kelly.

Above all, my heart is overcome by gratitude to the Spirit of grace, whom I have felt guide me through this book in unforgettable ways. You are my Light and Hope, and the Crest of all truth. You are without a doubt my greatest Friend. May all who read this book be drawn like Moses closer to Your flames, which burn but do not destroy. May they see the smile on Your face and raise up their hearts like sails, expecting only Your goodness to blow forth.

Foreword

G od loves to sing and He loves to sing over you! If you will stop to listen you can hear His lyrics—it's the Song of the Ages! Nothing else can make you dance like the soul-moving words of Solomon's ballad. It describes a journey we all must take, where we leave the darkness of hiding behind walls of insecurity and come into the light of an endless day.

I'm so grateful that God hasn't given us the heavy burden of religion, for those burdens were removed 2,000 years ago. Instead, God has given us a Song to cast out every fear and fill in every need within our hearts. The words of Solomon's song move the soul and brighten our eyes. The Song of the Ages must be heard with all its intensity and power in the last days. Open your heart and you'll begin to hum its melody, an unchained melody of grace that kisses the soul.

In the last days of this age we can expect the grace of God to be magnified even as darkness seems to overtake the nations. There is a Bright Light shining into our hearts, which gives energy, passion, and movement to our lives. This light is the Light of Jesus, our Bridegroom. He comes to rescue His lovers and to unite our souls to His majesty. Closer He comes, leaping over the mountains of fear, coming near to everyone who calls upon Him. He comes singing a song of love to awaken us! Will we arise and leave our religious "walls" behind to run away with Him?

Nick Padovani has done a marvelous job in giving us the music sheet to the Song of the Ages. You'll love the way he unfolds the mysteries of Solomon's greatest of all songs. Hidden symbols will be unlocked in the pages of this book. I was personally delighted to read through the manuscript and find so many wonderful secrets made clear. The text is only understood by lovers of God, and Nick will not disappoint the true seekers. You will find a resting place, a hiding place, a glorious place of Eden's paradise as you read and enter in. Bring your heart into the fire of this message and you will burn with holy passion.

Get ready to have everything change as you dance to the lyrics of The Song of the Ages! You will never go back to dead religion again.

Dr. Brian Simmons
The Passion Translation Project

1 In the Beginning was a Song

The Song of Songs, which is Solomon's...
(1:1)

There are melodies that originate in the heart of the Maker, blasting like a trumpet from heaven and arriving sometimes as only a whisper in our hearts. These are the songs of eternity—glorious melodies that play over us even when distractions abound and the distorted sounds of the earth try to drown them out. These are the eternal songs and messages that continue to play all around us, calling out to those with ears to hear and eyes to see. And in the midst of it all, there is a Great Song. A Song to which all of heaven calls us to tune in. A Song that trumps every other. In fact, every good song is but a distant echo of this one.

This is the Song of the Ages.

It is a Song that an anointed king from Israel captured in allegory and poetry thousands of years ago. It is the truest Song, and all others find their origin and destiny in it...

In the opening line of the Song of Solomon, an absolutely bold and radical statement is made. The writer, King Solomon, declares under the inspiration of the Holy Spirit that this is the "Song of songs." In other words, he professes that this is the Song of *all* songs. He does not say that this is the Song of all *his* songs (because he wrote quite a few—1005 to be exact). Nor does he say that this is the Song of all earthly songs—past, present or future

11

ones to come. Instead, he plainly declares that this is the Song of all songs, which would then include the unfathomable melodies of angels in heaven and any other spheres of existence there are beyond time and space. This is the Song of them all.

Thankfully, ours heart are built like antennas and we have the ability pick up the frequency of this all-encompassing melody. Yet it's an unfortunate fact of our journey that our hearts can also pick up many other frequencies, including those that have the potential to veil the beauty of this one. But as we learn to focus in, to listen beyond any discord or distraction, something powerful and effortless begins to happen. You too begin to sing...and celebrate...and dance. And there is no distraction that can take your joy away from you.

The following pages are simply an attempt to help you tune in. But before we get into this Song—the greatest Song—let's pause for a moment and discuss something entirely different...

Strings of the Universe

At the smallest level of matter there is nothing but energy. In other words, if you were to keep zooming in on any substance in the universe, whether the arm of your chair or a rock on the moon, you would eventually find just raw energy. In fact, it is energy moving at different levels of vibration that gives form and substance to the physical things around us. In many sectors of the scientific community these tiny vibrations are known as "strings." They are the strings upon which notes play, thus giving form and substance to everything there is. Through a collection of these subatomic musical notes, the universe moves and manifests. These musical notes—the vibrating strings that make up matter—compose the very symphony of the universe in all of its different shapes, colors, and forms.

In the midst of these discoveries of the subatomic world even atheistic and agnostic scientists have referred to these forces as the mind of God. Whether they would admit it or not, this ultimately gives evidence to the fact that *in the beginning, the Lord spoke.* Creation was brought forth by the Word of the Father.

In the beginning was the Word, and the Word was with God, and the Word was God ... All things came into being through Him.
(Jn. 1:1, 3)

I want to set some wider context for what you're about to read, which is somewhat of a commentary on an ancient text, but more so a call to tune in to something eternal and life-changing. If the Father spoke and there came forth all the majestic forces of this physical universe, then one can imagine that the words and lyrics of His greatest Song would indeed bring creative substance and form as well. Hence, when we learn to tune our hearts to this music, it will play its melody upon the very strings within us, and a harmony and beauty will emerge within our very souls.

I am not trying to make some overly scientific hypothesis as to the importance of this Song. I only mean to point out that we are to be hearers of the Word. As the apostle Paul said, it is not those who "obey the law" who see the miracle-working power of the Spirit in their lives, rather it is those who simply "hear the Word" with faith (see Gal. 3:1-3). There is a lot of disharmony and chaos in this world, because people are listening to the wrong "sounds," which are often just corrupted note-changes from the original Song. This can be likened to when Paul warned about listening "to a different Gospel—which is really no Gospel at all" (Gal. 1:6-7 NIV). Yet God is calling His people to wake up and hear His original music...and then go out and dance before a sleeping world.

At this very moment, there is an awakening that the Lord desires to bring forth in the earth. In fact, it's already been happening for a long time. This is an awakening to the full glory of Christ and the reality of our union with Him—the One who is in perfect harmony with the Father. As already said, this book only seeks to help tune our ears to listen to this wondrous music so that it might awaken our own souls in a fresh and vibrant way.

The Song of the Lamb

It is quite clear that the Song of Solomon is an allegory between the Lord Jesus and His people. Jesus is called the "Son of David" throughout the New Testament because He was the true heir of King David's throne who would reign in peace and righteousness. Solomon was David's natural son and was a shadow and type of Christ. So, on the one hand, this Song could be called the "Song of the Son of David." And yet Christ is also called the "Lamb of God" in Scripture (Jn. 1:29). So, on the other hand, this could also be called the "Song of the Lamb." For the Lamb and the Son of David are one in the same. This was ultimately not Solomon's Song, but the Lamb's Song, Jesus Christ.

I have a suspicion that there is a strong connection between this Song and the one sung by the saints in Revelation, which is called the "Song of the Lamb" (see Rev. 15:3). Creation was originally brought forth by the Word of the Father (and we know that the Word is Jesus Christ—*in the beginning* Jesus was the One to bring forth life and substance to the universe). At the end of the age, all of creation will then join together with His voice, revealing a complete redemption and a perfect harmony. As the book of Revelation reveals, the Lamb's Song is truly the climax of the story that God is telling. This is a melody that is already being played out in creation, but it will reach its crescendo with the revelation of the union between Christ and His beloved Bride. It is the joining of God and His children in perfect synchronicity.

I believe that as the very vibrations and melodies of His Song penetrate our hearts, everything will be revolutionized. Like the Word that proceeded from the mouth of God and birthed galaxies and gravity, this Song from the Father's heart will birth the fullness of life and liberty in the hearer. It will bring about the true glory and manifestation of His sons and daughters. The universe itself is groaning for mankind to come into harmony with Christ, its "strings" thus playing the Song of the Lamb throughout every corner of earth and space. The world may appear to be playing a tune that has struck absolutely horrible notes throughout its existence. This is because sin has brought a crashing disruption in the original melodies the Lord had intended to ring through creation. Nonetheless, the Lord has and will turn this cacophony into a symphony of incredible glory.

A Song for the Reformation

Before we attempt to dive into this glorious text and turn the antenna of our hearts to the story that it tells and the melodies that it sings, I want to draw your attention to something else. Over the course of history, certain books of the Bible have provided incredible truth and relevance to certain things that the Holy Spirit was highlighting at that point in time. For example, the book of Isaiah was replete with revelation which the early church utilized to speak to their generation about the suffering Messiah. In the 1500s, the books of Romans and Galatians carried timely messages that were unpacked during the Protestant Reformation. And some dormant truths and realities in the book of Acts became very influential and relevant during the fresh moves of the Holy Spirit that began to stir at the turn of the 20th century.

I believe that we are in the midst of a reformation unlike any before. It is a building upon previous reformations, and eventually it will not even be defined as a "reformation." The words "restoration" and "reality" will most likely be the more appropriate terms for it. Now the bold statement that I would like to make is that the Song of Solomon is and will be one of the key books that bring forth the light and revelation needed in order to see this restoration in full momentum—just as Galatians or Acts were pivotal in previous times. Indeed, many leaders in the Body of Christ are beginning to tap into this book's fresh message for the world today. But we have only scratched the surface of this book's contents. The Lord has plans to show us even more of the heights and depths of its words.

With that being said, we need to remember that reformations can often come with great offense. In the days of Christ, when He walked upon the earth, the offensive revelation that came forth was the revealing of the Son of God. The people of Israel, even the most astute teachers of the Scriptures, barely had a grid for the unveiling of God's beloved Son. I believe there is an offensive and mind-blowing revelation coming to the earth yet again in the years preceding Christ's second coming. A revelation that even some of the greatest teachers of the Scriptures today may have no grid for—and, unfortunately, may initially reject.

And that is the revelation of the beloved *sons* of God.

Or, to borrow from the words of the apostle John, the "Bride of Christ." The one who is equally yoked and united with the Holy One.

This of course is not a "new" revelation any more than the Son of God was truly a new revelation for the people of Israel. The Christ was hidden in types and shadows in Scriptures all along and was always existent as the eternal Word of God. In similar fashion, the full and glorious church has always existed in the heart of God (even though she was created while Christ is eternal). She may not be the theme of the Scriptures in the same way that Christ is, but she is certainly the theme of His heart and the joy that was set before Him in His death. Therefore, you can be sure that she too has been hidden in the Scriptures as well.

Solomon's Song is a book that speaks of the union between Christ and His Bride—a union that was already sealed on the cross. The unveiling of this Song will thus help prepare and teach us to walk in the fullness of Christ's love and authority. For it will show us that our union with Christ goes far deeper than what man's teachings could ever conjure up or water down. Our union with Christ is the fuel that will drive the "emerging church" on the horizon. When I say *emerging*, I am not referring to some cool postmodern movement of spirituality. I am talking about a Bride rising and shining like the dawn in the full awareness of her Bridegroom's love, dancing without hesitation to the Song that

He sings over her. Therefore, this is a reformation—a restoration—that will trump every other. In fact, every past reformation is but a distant echo of this one.

A Final "Note"

As you read this book it will be important to understand the method of interpretation being used. The book is being interpreted allegorically in the rabbinical tradition of *sod*. This was considered one of the greatest methods of interpreting Scripture, which was that of allegory, parable, and discovering the hidden meaning to the ancient text. The apostle Paul was trained in the tradition of *sod* and it often shows up in his writings, such as Galatians when he discussed Hagar and Sarah, or in Ephesians when he discussed Adam and Eve. The writer of Hebrews utilized it when discussing Melchizedek, as did Peter when he wrote about Noah's flood in his first epistle. This is an uncovering of the shadows of the Old Testament, which were hidden messages that pointed to Christ.

God loves to speak in parables with hidden meaning. It was one of the main things Jesus did when He walked the earth. In fact, at one point, parables were the only way He taught. But the Song of Solomon is perhaps the most powerful parable of them all. Solomon himself wrote, "It is the glory of God to conceal a matter, but it is the glory of kings to search out a matter" (Prov. 25:2). God has concealed beautiful truths in His Word, including this mysterious Song, and it is the glory of His rising Kings and Queens to uncover and dive into its mysteries. Solomon, a king himself, was one to search out the deep things of God as he penned this text. As a royal priesthood, we now get to jump into that journey as well.

So let's be clear about something. The Song of Songs is not a book giving good marital advice. That is the "cover" under which the glory of this book has been hidden in recent centuries. Somewhere along the line the evangelical church began to use this book as a guideline for sex and marriage. Now Scripture is multi-layered, so I'm sure there are wonderful truths to pick up in regards to earthly marriage. But that is not the point of this Old Testament text. Some of the greatest saints, leaders, and church mystics throughout history have absolutely adored the message in this book, because they recognized that it spoke to something much deeper. It speaks to the union between Jesus Christ and His church.

This book seeks to join in with the rising chorus throughout history that has echoed the universe-changing messages found in Solomon's Song. Read the following pages with an awareness of the Lord's love and guidance. Allow Him to take over as you read. May the Holy Spirit alone be the One to bring the notes and meaning of this Song to ring true in your own heart. As you move forward, may you also find confidence in your Maker's design of your heart. It is indeed an antenna custom built to pick up the frequencies of His love.

2 The Kiss of the Spirit

May he kiss me with the kisses of his mouth!
For your love is better than wine.
Your oils have a pleasing fragrance,
Your name is like purified oil;
Therefore the maidens love you.

Draw me after you and let us run together!
The king has brought me into his chambers.

We will rejoice in you and be glad;
We will extol your love more than wine.
Rightly do they love you!
(1:2-4)

When man was brought forth from the dust of the earth, something unimaginable took place. The Maker breathed into Adam's lungs by leaning into his very face and releasing His breath. To put it in other terms, the creation of man began with a kiss. A kiss that released the divine life of God within the clay of man's form.

The story of the Song of Solomon follows a young maiden from the land of Shulam and it begins with her a deep desire for that same kiss of life. She longs for "the very Spirit-kiss of His mouth" (Sgs. 2:2b TPT). The Shulammite is revealed as one who is looking for the kiss that was breathed into Adam, which brought him into life in its fullest substance and deepest bliss—life as it was revealed in the Garden of Eden. Eden is the place of our origin and it speaks to the deepest truths concerning this thing we call "life." Within Eden, all the underlying motivations of religion and philosophy find their source, like pure spring water under layers of mud.

Eden was the place of unhindered fellowship with God. Along with this came a deep and transparent enjoyment of one another and with all of nature. It was a place of spontaneity, creativity, intimacy, adventure, and wonder. The skeptic would of course relegate this kind of life to the realm of fairy tale and myth, but our hearts know to challenge the skeptic's bark when the fleeting beauties of life hit us and we are confronted with the remembrances of Eden. Things such as family, fellowship, poetry, good food, adventure, and transcendent experiences are just a few examples. These elements testify to the truth of Eden like wind bringing a distant aroma of a far off but sure scent. At the beginning of her journey, the Shulammite is crying out for the Scent itself. She is looking for the Eden Life where man walked with God reflecting His perfect image and likeness. She is looking for redemption—not as an intellectual doctrine, but as a reality. She knows this comes from the kiss released by God's Spirit and breath.

At the onset of this story and Song, it needs to be said that the overall human story does not begin with original sin, but with original glory. We come from the essence of the Eternal, which is why Solomon told us in another one of his books that eternity is written into our hearts. We were in the very heart and Spirit of the Father before time began, and so He knew us quite well even before we were in our mother's womb. We were a dream in His heart that existed in the realm of eternity and we were brought forth into a specific point in time and space. This dream may have been knit together with atoms, cells, and flesh, but those are simply the complex paint strokes of an eternal portrait. A portrait with infinite value—*infinite* because the Infinite One finds value in it. This is where we come from, and it is ultimately where we are headed.

In the fall of Adam we obviously veered away from this original identity and portrait. We bought into a lie and allowed deception to darken our hearts and corrupt our behavior. We fell back into the "dust." As a result, we came to embrace a dust-based mentality and identity and began treating ourselves and one another as such. This is clearly at the heart of so many of the world's issues. Kings and dictators throughout the millennia have trampled upon whole people groups like dust to gain more money, land, and power. Violence and murder is itself a clear picture that we see another human as worthless dust and not as one made in the sacred image of God. To lust after another person and look at their body as a source of personal gratification is to relegate beauty as glittering dust to possess. Enslavement of one another is seeing only dust in our fellow man, which is to be used for our own enjoyment and prosperity. And to curse another man is to see dust and not glory.

We have forgotten the Rock from which we were hewn and the origin of our birth through the kiss of God. We have forgotten the awe and majesty of the Lord Himself, and in that forgetfulness we have forgotten ourselves. So the prophet Isaiah rightfully declares that we must *"rise out of the dust"* and *"sit enthroned"* in the original garments of glory with which we were created (see Isa. 52:2 NIV).

The Song of Solomon captures the journey of this young woman from Shulam who is following Isaiah's call. She represents those of us who are slowly awakening to the love of Christ, who know that there is more to their lives than a dust-based existence. Even though the original image and glory appears to be broken and shattered, this young woman calls out for a return—a redemption—to that original life. Throughout the Song, she will receive the answer to this opening prayer, and will eventually rise from the dust and sit enthroned in her identity as a child of God and a co-heir with Jesus Christ. She will take hold of this life and receive the Lord's glorious kiss.

We will find that the Shulammite is not content to just sit by and wait to die in order to experience Eden. She desires to take hold of it now. She, the rising Bride of Christ, is one who is aware of the *More* to life, religion, spirituality, and then some. She is tired of religious games and empty prophetic promises. She longs now for the kisses of His mouth—His Word—to awaken the life of His Spirit within her, which is indeed the life of her original design. The apostle Paul once commanded his young disciple and spiritual son to do the same thing. "Take hold of eternal life," he said to Timothy (1 Tim. 6:12).

At the beginning of her journey, we find the Shulammite to be much like a believer today who is looking for real "eternal life" (which, in the New Testament, can also be translated as the "Life of the Ages"). She is like a believer who wants to go beyond just "church-ianity" and behavior modification following a sinner's prayer. She has somewhat of an understanding that the term "eternal life" is actually referring to the Life of God (Eph. 4:18), and that eternal life is to actually know God in the here and now (see Jn. 17:3). The concept of eternal life in Scripture was never meant to be known as this thing found far out in the future. It is about a life lived now. Yes, this life will extend into all eternity, but that is just one benefit of the life we have currently been given in Christ.

Thankfully, this concept is being restored to the church like never before in our day. Therefore, the Song of Songs is becoming more applicable than ever. Many people today are challenging our fire insurance models of salvation, which has an unbalanced emphasis on a future hope in heaven. Such thinking is based upon a watered down view of the Scriptures, as well as unbelief in the full promises of God for our present lives. This unbelief has bred a Christianity based on gaining converts instead of bringing about a manifestation of the Kingdom on earth through those who are disciples of Christ.

There is so much more that could be said about this dilution of the concept of eternal life, but we will leave it at that for now. This young maiden is obviously someone who knows enough of Jesus to ask Him for life. But she is looking for real life, not just another pumped up motivational message that puts the promises of God far out in the future. She is looking for the abundant life that Jesus promised *now*, even in the midst of trial and difficulty. And not only is her journey centered on finding real life in and of itself, but it is all about finding this life in the context of love and intimacy.

Intimacy with God

Now it may be important to give a quick disclaimer at this point in the book. This journey through the Song of Solomon will address an intimacy with God that might be uncomfortable because of its symbolic connections to romance and sexuality. In fact, in ancient Israel, young Hebrew boys were not even allowed to read the Song of Solomon until a certain age. But we need to have some maturity here and understand that earthly romance and marriage are pictures of Something Greater. Even sex is simply a physical representation of a spiritual reality of union, worship, and divine ecstasy.

This is not to devalue the beauty of romance and marriage and say that it's just a "symbol." It is not just a symbol, but rather it is a *sacrament*, revealing something of eternity. And there is infinite value placed upon this revealing sacrament because it bears a message of eternal glory. Like an angel bringing a message from heaven, marriage and sex bear a heavenly message to be experienced in every sense of the body and soul. We should not worship the messenger, but we can appreciate its beauty and power. Marriage and romance are glorious avenues by which the world can tangibly and physically enter into something that cannot be communicated with simple chapters and verses. And when these concepts are embraced in their purest form of marital union, they yield incredible foretastes of eternal glory.

Nonetheless, these things are still signposts of a greater reality and so we can release some uncomfortable awkwardness with these connections between God and us. We are not talking about literal sexuality or an actual romantic journey. Jesus is not your boyfriend. All of this is especially important for men to get a handle on if they are to fully appreciate this book. We are both the "bride of Christ" and the "sons of God." These are all terms that speak to a greater relationship in the Scriptures. All of these things are just concepts meant to draw our attention to a relationship that is of the deepest love and beauty imaginable. So even though there is romantic language throughout this book, it is a language that speaks to a higher reality. Move beyond the image to the substance behind it and you will gain unbelievable insight and revelation from the Song.

Courtroom Drama or Eternal Love Story?

Throughout the Shulammite's journey, we will see very clearly that there is a great love story unfolding in the creation and redemption of humanity. The Song is actually a symbolic unveiling of the Gospel penetrating the human heart. Again, the Shulammite represents all of those who are on the journey to intimately know the Father, Son, and Spirit. This automatically shows us that the Gospel is a story of love more than anything else. Unfortunately, we have often misunderstood (or miscommunicated) this element of redemption.

This is an incredibly large issue to discuss, but suffice it to say that the church has been deeply (and often unknowingly) entangled with Greek and Roman thinking in its understanding of the Gospel. This thinking has subtly spread throughout the world and it has left us with a presentation of the Gospel that takes on more judicial and legal undertones than ones that embrace relationship and love. In fact, there are sadly many people who will not even read works by authors who speak on the emotional and romantic elements of Christianity, but prefer the so-called "meat" of more judicial and analytical approaches of breaking down the Scriptures. They look at the emotional and narrative shades of the Gospel as secondary to their legal and intellectual facts on things like justice, wrath, substitution, and other theological terms. What they do not realize, however, is how easy it is to live more out of pagan and Greek thought than the actual overarching messages of the Word.

The story of redemption is not so much about a cosmic court case as it is about a great love story. The young Shulammite is one who does not appear to have any time or interest for the legal interpretations of Scripture. Legal interpretations that might make for great Sunday School lessons and educational lectures but hold no authentic power in the face of real life. She, like many of us, is recognizing the impure mixture of Greek and Roman rationalism and is looking to break free into the fullness of the love story that is the Gospel. A love story that will propel her much further than any courtroom drama ever could.

Better Than Wine

In the third verse, the woman acknowledges that this love is far greater than any earthly pleasure. Wine is her example, which in Solomon's day was always associated with the heights of human pleasure and experience. Thus this love she is seeking brings a greater intoxication than anything this world could ever offer. Just as the Shulammite is done with unfulfilling and judicial interpretations of the Gospel, she is also done with the fruit of those interpretations: a dry and boring spiritual life. She is looking for real life in the context of eternal love that can only be compared to the intoxicating atmosphere found in Eden.

In the next verse, we learn that this life springs from the One whose "name is purified oil." This is speaking of none other than Jesus, the only One who can bring us the eternal life of God. Within the Scriptures, oil is most often a symbol and image of the Holy Spirit. Therefore, Jesus's very name—the fullness of His identity—is one and the same as the Holy Spirit. He is the One who releases the pleasure and joy of God in our lives. He is the very Wine of Heaven who bears the fruit of God's life within us. The Shulammite's journey and desire is not about taking hold of an experience, but about encountering a Person. It is this Person who brings us the true experience of Eden. This is something that will be explored more and more as the story progresses.

The Inner Chambers

When the Shulammite speaks of the King bringing her "into his chambers," this reveals a union of the most intimate kind. Indeed, this is a divine union, for the King is a symbol of Jesus Christ. Now in Solomon's day (and throughout history), the average person would never be able to enter into the inner chambers of a king. Such a place was reserved for his bride alone. Again, this speaks of an unsearchable union.

What is astounding is that the Song declares the truth of their union at the beginning of the story—well before the Shulammite actually goes on to experience it outwardly. Even before she experientially embraces her union and intimacy with the Lord in the later parts of the book, the Song declares that she already has this union right from the beginning. This is somewhat confusing until you understand the spiritual context of the journey and its overall connection to the story of redemption...

One of the greatest revelations of the ages is that our union with Christ was accomplished before the world was created. He is in fact "the Lamb who was slain before the foundation of the world" (Rev. 13:8). Like Eve who was hidden in Adam's side, the church was "in Christ" before time began (see Eph. 1:4). Even in knowing that we would descend into darkness, God confidently and excitedly created the human race with the knowledge of our redeemed innocence and identity in Christ. This identity would be revealed and accomplished through Jesus at the "fullness of time" (Gal. 4:4). In other words, this salvation was always present in eternity, but it was "revealed," or manifested, in physical time and space through Christ's work on the cross. (The following Scriptures are just some of many verses that communicate this timeless truth: Rom. 16:25-26, Eph. 1:4 & 3:11, 2 Tim. 1:9-10, Tit. 1:2, 1 Pet. 1:20.)

There is a story to this journey being played out, but make no mistake about it, the victory and "happy ending" is already sealed from the beginning. We were in the innermost chambers of Christ's heart even before we arrived in our mother's womb. Throughout the rest of this book, we will watch as the Shulammite comes into the intimacy and freedom she desires to find in the kiss of God's Spirit and Word. In the next section of the Song, we will find the Shulammite seemingly a million miles away from it. Yet here in the beginning we see a reference to a union and love that has already taken place. This is a work that was already completed (see Heb. 4:3), but throughout the Song it will get revealed (or "worked out," as Paul says in Philippians 2:12). And so her story and our own should begin with nothing less than confidence and joy.

Rejoicing, Gladness, and Normal Christianity

Speaking of joy, the Shulammite follows her discussion on the inner chambers by saying, "We will rejoice in you and be glad!" At the end of the fourth verse, we see that these revelations and encounters of His love will lead only to rejoicing and gladness. Joy and gladness are indeed the fruits of salvation and of truly knowing God. As we continue to track with the Shulammite, we must be careful that we do not let any "mutilator of flesh" try to paint for us a Christianity of pain and depression. There is always suffering in this world due to love's call to embrace the least of these, but Christianity is a movement and celebration of joy more than anything else. In fact, joy is our truest strength.

In Acts 13, the apostles "suffer" physical persecution and pain. Yet right at the end of that chapter, it says that they got up from their persecution and were "continually filled with joy" (Acts 13:52). The key word there is *continually*. No persecution or trial can ever quench the river of love awakened in somebody who knows the life found in Christ. There is incredible joy found in this Gospel of Redemption, and we need to guard ourselves from those who would steal that joy and water down the message with legalism, fear, and other yokes of bondage.

Depression is not a fruit of the spirit, even if well-intentioned preachers have made a holy thing of it. "The less happy you are, the holier you are," is how the lie is subtly told (which often leads to false humility). But Jesus was anointed with the oil of joy above *all* His companions (Heb. 1:9). Yes, He was "a man of sorrows" according to Isaiah 53; however, that passage is primarily about His substitutionary work on our behalf. That is where we learn that He took our sin, our pain, and *our sorrows*, and bore them away on the cross. Isaiah 53 runs parallel to Isaiah 61 where God talks about replacing our mourning with the oil of joy. This is the passage Jesus announced at the beginning of His ministry and so came to fulfill—not just for heaven one day, but for the here and now. Thus, when He was resurrected, Jesus promised His disciples that no one would take their joy away from them. Why? Because He was forever crushing the power of depression and fear. Freedom from these things is a living reality based upon the power of Christ's resurrection.

The church has often exalted sorrow, suffering, and death (the mutilating of the flesh) when the major themes of our faith are actually defined by love, joy, and peace in the Kingdom of God (see Rom. 14:17). As the Shulammite grows in the joy found in her union with Christ, this rejoicing and gladness will only multiply and increase. She will go on to fulfill the desire that Jesus and the apostles had for all the believers they oversaw—which was to be made *complete in joy* (see Jn. 15:11, 2 Cor. 1:24, 1 Pet. 1:8, 1 Jn. 1:4).

So this is the beginning of the Shulammite's journey, as well as all those who would take hold of the Life of the Ages found in Christ. She is looking for a life of love that is greater than the intoxications of this world—one that leads to an overflow of gladness, joy, and peace. Mere head-knowledge is not enough. A dry and boring spirituality is no longer relevant. The Shulammite is looking for the life of her origin in Eden, an origin that goes back even before the Garden to the very heart of the Trinity. She looks for a greater manifestation of what has already been sealed from all eternity.

3 Dark or Lovely?

Dark am I
Yet lovely,
daughters of Jerusalem.
Dark like the tents of Kedar
Like the tent curtains of Solomon.

Do not stare at me because I am dark,
because I am darkened by the sun.
My mother's sons were angry with me
and made me take care of the vineyards;
my own vineyard I had to neglect.
(1:5-6 NIV)

The journey to Eden has a beginning point that is quite telling. Here we find a simple dialogue between the Shulammite and the Lord. In this opening dialogue we will find the very root issue of why the seeker is not experiencing the life she desires. The Shulammite has asked for a return to Eden. She knows Jesus came to seek and save *that which was lost*. Eden is what was lost, and so she is taking Him at His Word. Yet in the very beginning we come to something extremely important. We come first to her view of herself and a question of her identity. This is revealed through this powerful exchange of conversation between her and Jesus.

"I am dark," she begins. But right then, there is a Divine Interruption to her self-defeating comment.

"But you are lovely."

She argues back with this Voice. The Shulammite says, "I am like the tents of Kedar."

The Voice responds. "You are like the curtains of Solomon."

Many commentators have wrongfully missed the dialogue in these opening verses. They have assumed that this is one long contradictory statement of the Shulammite describing herself. Originally there were no scripted directions in the initial manuscripts as far as who was speaking and when. Therefore, interpreters have had to add their own opinions as far as who is speaking throughout the text. Peruse different Bible translations and you will see varying opinions about who is speaking at which point in the story. Of course, some dialogue is open to interpretation, but it is vitally important that we get this particular exchange correct, because it sets the stage for so much of what is to come. This is an actual argument between her and the Lord which ends up revealing a core issue within her heart. This very dialogue is where many of us will find ourselves when we seek the fullness of life that we were designed to experience.

Here is what is happening. At this point in her story, the young maiden is still identifying with a sinful nature, or her "flesh." She sees herself as "dark" and therefore stands in a position of shame, which is clearly seen when she asks the Lord to not stare at her imperfections. One might think of Adam and Eve when they first began to lose the Eden life. They hid shamefully in the bushes and covered themselves with fig leaves. This shame draws a parallel with much of the church throughout its history and can be seen in the lives of many of God's saints today. There is an identification with sinfulness amongst God's people, which the Gospel tells us we should no longer have because of the work of Christ. The 10th chapter of Hebrews clearly teaches this when it says that we are not to even have a "consciousness of sins."

But like he does with the Shulammite, the Lord calls to us today and declares us as "lovely." Darkness is not the truth about who we really are. The Lord sees and understands this truth, because it is through His death that He has forever circumcised the "sinful nature" away from us (see Col. 2:11). Circumcision is a powerful analogy. When literal foreskins were cut and circumcised, the Israelites did not keep them hanging around their necks like some decorative ornament. It was discarded completely—and it was forgotten. It was gone.

It is the same with our sinful nature through Christ's work on the cross. We can no longer identify with a sinful nature, because according to the Lord, it's just not there anymore. This is clearly what the sixth chapter of Romans also teaches. We died to sin in the death of Christ and it is a past tense reality. It does not say that we were made *numb* to sin's power or given a boost of Christian adrenaline to stand against it. It definitively and explicitly says we *died to sin*. This speaks of the utmost finality.

Anybody who teaches that we still need to crucify our sins is not reading the New Testament correctly. In its original Greek language, there is no such existence of re-crucifying sins. When the Scriptures say to "mortify your flesh," this is better translated as "*consider as dead* the members of your flesh," as the New American Standard and other translations render it (see Col. 3:5). In other words, realize that your sinful nature is already crucified and put away!

There is a similar misinterpretation of Jesus's call for us to pick up our cross. "Picking up your cross" is not about your commitment to finish a job that Jesus only halfway completed. Rather, it is a simple commitment to follow Jesus no matter what persecution comes your way while in the meantime you enjoy your complete salvation from sin. Similarly, when John the apostle says, "If we say that we have no sin, we are deceiving ourselves" (1 Jn. 1:8), he is talking about those who reject their need for a Savior. Everyone in this world has sinned and needs a Savior. But when you come to the Savior, John later says, "he who is born of God does not sin" (1 Jn. 3:9 NKJV)!

Unfortunately, the Shulammite does not yet believe this. She argues back by comparing herself to the "tents of Kedar." These tents were the animal-skin shelters set up by the nomadic tribes of Kedar. These tents would bake and crack in the sun and as a result would become worn, blackened, and hard. Interestingly, Kedar is also one of the sons of Ishmael, which further emphasizes the meaning of this passage. The sons (or fruit) of Ishmael can clearly be identified with the sinful nature.

The fourth chapter of Galatians spells this out with utmost clarity in its comparison between Hagar, the mother of Ishmael, and Sarah, the mother of Jacob. One corresponds to the flesh while the other corresponds to the Spirit. Therefore, the Shulammite is comparing herself to a son of Ishmael, the sinful and corrupt nature that is darkened and hard. She is still identifying with the old covenant hardness and deceptiveness of her heart, instead of the new covenant truth that her heart is now new and pure.

So once again, the Lord disagrees with this statement and comes back with the most glorious and beautiful reply. He says to this self-loathing girl that she is in fact comparable to the fine linen curtains found in Solomon's temple. These are the very curtains of Solomon that surrounded the Holy of Holies! If we could grasp the significance of this statement, it would revolutionize everything we thought we knew about ourselves.

Jesus is comparing this young woman to the very garments that surrounded the Most Holy Place, which was the habitation of God's manifest presence and glory. Jesus calls out her identity right from the beginning as one who is a beautiful temple that hosts the glory of God, saying that her body and her overall being is like the fine linen curtains that surrounds the glory of God's being. Her heart is pure and any darkness she sees has sunk to the bottom of the seafloor. Interestingly, in verse five, He says this to her and to *all* the "daughters of Jerusalem." So this truth is for every one of us!

The End of the Sinful Nature

This is a book about adventure, freedom, and life; however, if we do not get a correct understanding about the circumcision or the complete removal of the sinful nature, we will have a very difficult time following along. This issue is undeniably a stumbling block that keeps God's people baking out in the sun (with occasional water breaks) instead of flourishing in the Promised Land with its overflowing fountains. It is the very first piece of dialogue between the Shulammite and the Lord and it is the first issue that the Lord addresses with us when we move forward spiritually, emotionally, and physically.

Basically, this whole issue gets at the root of a misunderstanding and a heresy in the church that goes back to the earliest days of Christendom. It is the identification with a sinful nature and a dualistic view of ourselves. Half-flesh, half-spirit. Half-evil, half-good. A deceitfully wicked heart and a new and purified heart. This dualistic view has its roots in Gnosticism and is not a part of the original Gospel that the apostles heralded. Gnosticism was a heresy that viewed the body as evil, and therefore it created a theology that says we will only be free from sin when we die and exit the physical body. But to borrow from the words of the 19th century theologian Adam Clarke, this crowns death as our savior and not Jesus—whose blood alone cleanses us from *all* unrighteousness.

People will often bring up Romans 7 as an argument against this. Many will say that Paul, in that chapter, is admitting to an internal battle of the flesh and spirit, where he can't do the things he wants to do because of indwelling sin. There is a centuries old debate over whether or not Paul is talking about himself in the present, or what his life was like before finding freedom in Christ. While the humble position might be to say that it is too controversial and we simply do not know the answer, this is actually dangerous ground to tread. A clear reading of Romans 7 in context is all that is needed to dispel this argument since Paul is speaking to those who know the law, and is thus explaining the experience and understanding of one under the law.

When you are living legalistically and constantly trying to clean yourself up (or re-crucifying your flesh), you will always run into a wall with the feeling that you can never do what you want to do. This is because "the letter kills, but the Spirit gives life" (2 Cor. 3:6). When you live according to the law, you are living out of your own efforts. This is what is sometimes referred to as the "self-life." It is not that your "self" is intrinsically bad, but rather that the self was never made to operate independently from the Spirit of God. Living under the law entails living in such an independent manner, for you are trying to attain to His nature by your own efforts. Yet anything outside of union and trust in God leads one into the realm of deception, which is a breeding ground for darkness and sin.

Dualism—the teaching of two natures within—stems from Plato and earlier pagan thinkers and has no place in the teachings of the apostolic Gospel. Pastors, prophets, and laymen will often teach on the story of two "dogs" within. One dog is evil (which represents your sinful nature) and the other is good (which represents your spirit). Whichever "dog" you feed more is the one who will win the fight. Therefore, if you feed your spirit with things like prayer, fasting, and Bible study, you will win the battle against the flesh. However, if you feed your flesh with television and pizza, then your little spirit dog is going to whimper out and lose.

What many of these teachers don't realize is that they are actually borrowing a Native American proverb about two inner wolves, which is rooted in pagan dualistic philosophy and not in the revelation of the finished work of Jesus Christ. The apostle Peter told us "to abstain from sinful desires, which war against your soul" (1 Pet. 2:11 NIV). He did not say that sinful desires wage war *in the soul*. This faulty understanding of a remaining sinful nature sets us up for a never-ending battle with an ominous "flesh" that really can't be won until we die. It looks to self-discipline as the savior from sin (which leads to utter frustration and burn-out), and not to Jesus and His blood.

Galatians 5 is the next thing that the enemy uses in keeping us from seeing that our sin is actually "taken away." (If you remember, John the Baptist said the Lamb of God came to take away our sins... It should then be no surprise to us that the Lamb was actually successful at this!) Galatians 5, which talks about the flesh and the spirit, is actually making the point to say that the flesh, or sinful nature, has no place in the life of a believer. The two natures do not go together. They are "contrary to one another," it says.

In fact, the chapter closes up by saying that "those who belong to Christ Jesus *have crucified the sinful nature with its passions and desires*" (Gal. 5:24). This puts the final nail in the coffin on this issue since it is not a chapter about two natures within. Paul teaches that these things do not go together and he is giving the Galatians their death certificate for the old man. He is calling them away from the self-life of the law into a life of trusting in their identity in Christ. He ultimately reminds them that they are new creations, and that this new creation truth is all that really matters (see Gal. 6:15).

Someone might ask, "If we no longer have a sinful nature then why do we still sin?" This important question unfortunately stems from unbelief or perhaps an ignorance of the Gospel's complete message. It shows that we often want to interpret Scripture through our experience, instead of allowing Scripture to illuminate and change our experience. Nonetheless, it is still a valid and significant subject that must be addressed.

I'll first answer this question with another question... Why did Adam and Eve first sin when they were without a sinful nature? They sinned before "sin entered into the world" (Rom. 5:12). Think about it. They were in a perfect condition and were completely innocent. Yet an outside force waged war against their soul. They were told a lie, and this deception led to mistrust which brought about the fruit of darkness. It is the same with an innocent and redeemed believer today. They have the very nature of

Christ, but deception and mistrust can still lead to incredible rebellion, like it did with Adam and Eve.

This is why Paul constantly teaches about being *rooted and established in the faith* and the *renewing of the mind*. In fact, you are "transformed by the renewing of your mind" (Rom. 12:2). We still sin because our minds have not been fully renewed to the truth of our freedom. A hostile world can still play on our God-given desires and corrupt our behavior through deception. But this does not change the core truth of who we are as the redeemed sons and daughters of God. When we drink the milk of the Word (the message of the Gospel and our complete freedom from sin), we will "grow in our salvation" (see 1 Pet. 2:1). As a result, we will walk out the freedom and holiness we already have. This basic truth is hidden all throughout Scriptures, but Gnosticism and Platonic dualism has polluted our ability to see it.

The question of why we still sin will ultimately be answered by going further along in the Shulammite's journey. She too does not believe the audacious good news of her true identity in Christ. As a result of her unbelief, darkness has become her outward experience. Nonetheless, the light of truth will begin to dawn upon her and she will start to experience the full truth of the Gospel. And this will happen to all of us as we follow the Lord in the paths of truth and grace that He is leading us on.

I am being very purposeful in looking more deeply at this opening dialogue between the Shulammite and the Lord. The question of whether we are dark or lovely is a pivotal starting point in our journey. We need to understand the foundation of what the cross accomplished and the reality of our co-crucifixion with Christ. Some will unfortunately cling to an argument that continues to identify with indwelling sin, which they will feel is their responsibility to crucify—instead of Jesus's already accomplished responsibility. They will hold onto that indwelling "dark side" and will keep baking out in the sun of religious striving as a result. This keeps countless people on the treadmill of religion and self-help modules in an effort to clean themselves up. Through it all, they end up interpreting Scripture through their own experience of sinfulness, instead of allowing the clear revelation of Scripture to trump their experience.

But for those who want to move forward in their journey to experience real life, we must at least begin to open up to the idea that we are now as white as snow (despite what we see and feel in the natural realm). Being "washed," "set free," and "redeemed" are not nice, motivational, pump-you-up phrases that the Bible gives to you so that you can have a wishy-washy hope of freedom one day. They are literal and true statements. We are free. Our hearts are washed clean. We are redeemed (or brought back to our original identity as the pure sons and daughters of God). This is true. And when we start to believe it, we will experience it.

Everything changes as this revelation hits us and we get rid of our self-loathing and depraved viewpoints of ourselves. It will take a while for the Shulammite to let go of this thinking and it might take some time for some of us as well. But the Lord is committed to letting this Truth be heard and experienced, even if unbelief stands in the way at this point.

Burnt Out By Religion

The Shulammite goes on to explain why she feels and looks the way she does. She attributes her experiences of sinfulness and hardness to her "labor under the sun." She then begins to talk about her mother's sons...

Scripture will often interpret Scripture. This is the best way to unpack the meaning behind parabolic symbols in a story like the Song of Solomon. It doesn't take much biblical knowledge to realize that the "Shepherd" and the "King" in this story is Jesus. However, it might take a little bit more study to see that the "mother" actually represents Mother Israel. And, for the New Testament believer, we can see that she ultimately represents Mother Church. Therefore, her "mother's sons" are religious leaders who have forced her into heavy labor out in the sun.

So in other words, the Shulammite is burnt out...by religion.

She says that she has neglected her own vineyard, which is the place of her own intimacy, identity, and rest before the Lord. This has happened (probably very subtly) because she has been working in other people's vineyards instead of her own. She has been busy doing "church" work, but has neglected the place of peace and rest in Christ. She has also labored under the false teaching of needing to clean herself up and crucify the flesh continually, which was already discussed.

In recent decades, there has been a much-needed shift in understanding intimacy with God as the starting place to true ministry. The beauty of this Song has begun to play its tune throughout the Body of Christ and the volume has been turned up like never before. People are realizing that they are sons and daughters before they are workers or servants. Nonetheless, a lot of damage has been done, and in many sectors of the church there are people who are still afraid to keep rest and intimacy as a priority over their work in the vineyard.

The problem is that many leaders are holding the sheep at gunpoint with powerful ammunition. Their weapon is the Bible and their bullets are select Scriptures used to intimidate and guilt the flock into a life of "hard service." As a result, people are busier than ever, but the fruits of peace and joy are frequently absent. Many teachers and leaders will minimize the plethora of Scriptures that speak about joy, rest and faith. They will acknowledge them of course, but will then quickly throw out the word "balance" in order to ensure the flock doesn't get too happy and too restful in the Lord. God forbid somebody serves Jesus purely out of love with no motivation of guilt or robotic religious duty! (I understand this is a tremendous generalization, but it is sadly filled with a lot of truth when you survey the vineyards throughout Christendom.)

Tell me, O you whom my soul loves,
Where do you pasture your flock

Where do you make it lie down at noon?
For why should I be like one who veils herself
beside the flocks of your companions?
(1:7)

And so the Bride looks for rest...

The Shulammite is no longer interested in religious, guilt-driven labors that only burn her out and leave her running in a constant sin-repentance-sin cycle. She is looking for that real Eden life of freedom. This is a life of inner rest, and it is the rest that Jesus promised to all who would come to Him. This is the rest that David experienced and penned in the 23rd Psalm where he related himself to a sheep who is made to lie down in green pastures. We were never meant to just talk and pontificate about such rest. Instead, we are called and designed to experience it in everyday life in a tangible and fragrant way.

Hidden in this request is also the Shulammite's desire to find complete righteousness (or the "loveliness" that the Lord declared over her earlier). She hopes to lie down at midday—or noon—which is a strong allusion to the Proverb that speaks about our righteousness shining forth like the noonday sun (Prov. 4:18). As you can see, the Shulammite is looking to lie down and experience a complete rest and a complete righteousness. In fact, the words *righteousness*, *rest*, and the *Eden life* are all different facets of the same diamond. A diamond that Jesus has freely given His church.

The Lord has already begun to speak the truth to her. It is hidden right in the beginning of the Song. This is the truth about her identity and that she already has everything she craves. This mystery has been revealed through the apostles all throughout their teachings. John said, "Of His fullness we have all received" (Jn. 1:16). Paul said that we are "complete in Christ" (Col. 2:10). Peter said, "We have been given everything that pertains to life and godliness" (2 Pet. 1:3). But it is God's pleasure to *reveal* this Mystery to His saints. It is one thing to hear the truth, like the Shulammite does in the beginning of this Song. It is a whole other thing to *know the truth*, for it is knowing the truth that leads to freedom.

And so now the Shepherd will bring her on an adventure to discover the riches she already possesses—that diamond of infinite beauty and value. With a gentle and kind heart, the Lord responds to His Bride's plea and will lead her into an intimate fellowship with His heart. He will respond by kissing her with His very *Word of Truth*.

4 The Way

If you yourself do not know,
Most beautiful among women,
Go forth on the trail of the flock
And pasture your young goats
By the tents of the shepherds.

To me, my darling, you are like
My mare among the chariots of Pharaoh.
Your cheeks are lovely with ornaments,
Your neck with strings of beads.

We will make for you ornaments of gold
With beads of silver.
(1:8-10)

Through the words of the prophet Hosea, the Lord once gave remarkable insight as to why His people suffer defeat and live outside of the place of rest and righteousness. It is a surprisingly simple statement, but under its surface lie waters of wisdom that run deeper than the earth.

"My people are destroyed for lack of knowledge" (Hos. 4:6).

Centuries later, the apostle Paul outlined the main goal of leadership in the church and expressed his chief hope for the future of God's people. This goal and hope was that one day all would come into "the full and accurate *knowledge* of the Son of God" (Eph. 4:13 AMP).

As the archetype and representative of God's people, the young Shulammite finds herself lacking knowledge that is keeping her from flourishing. "If you yourself do not *know*," the Lord says to her. Now we need to be clear that this is not simple "head knowledge." She may intellectually "know" the way to rest and righteousness, but she is obviously lacking the type of intimate knowledge that Paul and Hosea wrote about. It is this kind of knowledge that will need to come forth deep within her heart and it is exactly why the journey from here on out is even necessary.

Now before discussing the Lord's opening response to this lack of knowledge, I want to pause and just stand in awe of something. We are not just looking at *what* He says to her next, but *how* He says it. She is obviously one of those who are "perishing" under the burning of the sun. She is being "destroyed for lack of knowledge." Yet in His opening reply to her, He refers to the Shulammite as the "most beautiful among women." When we sit back and inhale the kindness and gentleness behind His words— words of instruction and correction—it is absolutely breathtaking.

This will perhaps give us deeper understanding into Jesus's heart when we read the more stern passages of Scripture. For instance, when He intensely cries "woe" upon Jerusalem, our hearts are enlightened to see that in the same breath He also spoke about His tender desire to gather Jerusalem to safety like a mother hen gathers her chicks (Mat. 23:37). Perhaps our hearts will soften when we read Jesus's strong rebuke of the Laodicean church in Revelation, whom He only rebukes because of His intense and unfailing love for them (Rev. 3:19).

How many shepherds have looked at "perishing" churches and individuals and have spoken to them across pulpits and air-waves in words of anger and condemnation. They can hide their religion behind the excuse that it's "righteous anger" or "tough love," but my simple question is this: where are the shepherds who look at the perishing Bride and refer to them as *the most beautiful among women*? These are words of incredible hope and affirmation even in her outwardly "dark" and perishing state.

So it is with unrelenting mercy and kindness that the Lord begins to call her forth into all the riches of the *grace and knowledge* of Jesus Christ...

Follow the Trail

Interestingly, the first thing Jesus encourages her to do is to continue to follow in the footsteps of the flock. In other words, He calls the Shulammite to follow in the footsteps of those who have gone before her in the paths of faith and grace. "Go forth on the trail of the flock," He says.

This is indeed a communal journey we are on and there is much to learn from those who have gone ahead of us. He is calling her here to look at the examples of others, and to remain teachable and humble along the way. This is absolutely vital in any journey forward. We can learn incredible truths about our identity and the finished work of Jesus Christ, but without remaining teachable and humble, we can easily lose our focus. This cannot be stressed enough at the early stages of this journey. There are deep truths of reformation and restoration at hand. But for those who catch these truths, we need to always remember the importance that we still don't have it all figured out. Unbelievable freedom is found by admitting this.

The Good Shepherd then gives her another important piece of advice. He reminds her to continue feeding her "young goats." Here, the Lord is asking her to not lose sight of her good responsibilities, especially her nurturing of the young. Many times when someone gets extreme revelations from heaven there is a temptation to "abandon all" and leave everything behind. This is a beautiful thing in one sense and yet a dangerous thing in another. The unfulfilled life of dry religion quickly loses its luster, which is good, but sometimes people can throw the baby out with the bathwater. They isolate themselves from certain things that God never intended we leave behind. So wisdom is needed here. There is always a shedding of old things as we take this deep dive into grace and allow our lives' responsibilities to be love-driven. But this needs to come with great wisdom and care.

At this point in the journey, the Bride lacks the "knowledge of God" or the "knowledge of truth" that we find discussed in so many places throughout His Word. And so the Lord is going to bring her into that place. However, he first encourages her to remain teachable, to learn from others who have grown in grace, and to keep nurturing those in her care. Establishing her in these basic words of wisdom, the answer to her longings begins to emerge...

The Crown Jewel of Creation

And of course the answer is never a textbook response. The answer is written in the melody of a Song from heaven, and we need to listen with the ears of our heart as much as with the ears of our head. As we do this, we find that a shift happens at this point of the Song. The Lord turns from giving her some initial instructions and begins expressing praise and adoration towards her. The Lord begins singing over His questioning companion and He does this by comparing her to a mare among Pharaoh's chariots.

To any young lady or man in Israel, a reference to the chariots of Pharaoh would immediately bring one particular image to mind—that of the Israelites at the Red Sea and the great Egyptian army approaching them from behind. Now imagine yourself in that scene. Standing before you is a large and shimmering sea, and right behind you lies a great open expanse of desert and hills. As you look back at that open expanse you first hear the ground shaking and the roaring echo of man and beast. As you continue to listen and the sounds grow, there slowly emerges the greatest army the world had ever known at that point in history. Complete with colorful banners, shimmering chariots, and soldiers of all kinds, this was an army of incomparable strength.

Let's take our imagination further and picture a beautiful mare standing front and center of this emerging army. Royal, stately, and breathtaking, few things could compare to the sight of that mare standing before this mass of chariots and warriors. Now casting aside the fear and panic you would feel in that position as an Israelite, just imagine the sheer glory of that sight. If we were to behold such a view it would absolutely take our breath away.

This, beloved of God, is the very feeling the Lord has when He sees us—the crown jewel of His creation. We are like the glorious appearing of a royal mare in the midst of a bannered army. This dimension of our beauty in God's eyes will be seen over and over again in the Song along with the fact that we take God's breath away. As we progress, the strength of this truth will be more intimately developed. This part of the Song is only the beginning of its unraveling to the searching Bride.

Jesus is wooing the Shulammite to His love and is speaking words that are beyond her present comprehension. Even before He explains more about His work on the cross, He wants her to know the motivation of love and beauty behind it. Jesus did not die for us out of a dry obligation to cosmic justice. Instead, it was an exhilarating movement of passion and joy for the beauty of His beloved creation. It is one thing to understand what Jesus did at the cross, but it is a whole other thing to know *why* He did it.

Nourishing Words of Heaven

He goes on to comment further on her appearance and the beautiful adornments that are upon her. You will see such praise and adoration time and time again throughout the Song. Part of the Bride's journey is simply hearing and receiving the Word of Truth. This is our journey as well—to be renewed in the deepest parts of our minds with the kiss of God's Word. People talk all the time about the importance of having God's Word in their hearts. They are usually referring to certain hopeful promises in the Scriptures. Now those hopeful promises are great to know and memorize, but they can become powerless if we don't understand the aspect of the Word that reveals the Lord's thoughts and feelings towards us—the very reason why those promises were spoken in the first place. This is the element of His Word that reveals what He knows to be true about us. It is in fact a deep and central part of the "knowledge of God." It is *His knowledge of us!*

The way to rest and righteousness is not some distinctive path of heavy discipline or self-mutilation. If that were the case, then all the religions of the world would have a piece of the market in getting us to the place our hearts long for. Discipline is a necessary part of life, but it is something that flows from a greater reality. The Shulammite will discover that the "way" actually involves becoming more intimately aware of God's love. It means that we know deep in our hearts the way that He feels about us—and what He knows to be true of us.

*This only would I learn of you, Received ye the Spirit by the works of the law, or by **the hearing** of faith?*
(Galatians 3:2 KJV)

We cannot stress this element of the journey enough as we venture deeper into the Song. Even in the place of failure and contradiction, we are to tune in to His Word and hear the Song of our Father. This is truly where some of our deepest growth will happen. For He looks at us and still calls us the most precious, breathtaking and pure thing that He has found in all of His creation... *Most beautiful,* He says. We are to rest and abide in this Word.

The prophet Ezekiel was once given a vision that communicates some of what we are talking about here. He saw a mighty river flowing forth from God's temple and wherever this river went, life came forth. He wrote, "every living creature that swarms in every place the river goes, will live" (Ez. 47:9). It is interesting to see that something could be living, but not truly *living.* Something can be moving and teeming in the waters of this world, but not truly alive. Ezekiel then saw great trees emerging from the riverbanks, which bore consistent and delicious fruit. We too are called to be trees planted by rivers of living water, bearing the fruit of the Spirit—the fruit of righteousness and rest.

Trees have a very simple formula for growth, and it does not involve toil and labor. It simply involves drinking in water, sun, and air. The Shulammite's journey, as well as our own, has a very similar formula. There is an organic element of growth in the knowledge of God that we cannot force or manipulate. We are like those trees that need to simply soak in the water of His Word and allow the sunlight of His grace to penetrate the bark of our minds. The wind of His Spirit is already there, and life will surely emerge. We will become "living creatures...that live."

Even when our leaves appear stunted in their growth and our branches are not as wide and strong as we would desire, the Lord sees the finished product. There is righteousness in the seed that gave us birth. And that seed is not high up in heaven in a theological land of make-believe. It is actually right in our own body and blood, and it releases a very real sap that flows through us. It is Christ in us, the hope of glory.

Though many people will not completely acknowledge it, the Word of God makes it quite clear that we are already righteous in Christ (see 2 Cor. 5:21 and read the rest of the epistles front to back). The work is finished and the job is done. This is more than just a "positional" reality. The word *positional* is often a nice concept used by theologians who do not always believe in the full promises of God and therefore put their true righteousness far away in heaven, safe and sound, away from the disappointing experience of present life. But righteousness has come and rest is available to all; not in the sweet by-and-by or in the golden streets of heaven, but right here in the cracked sidewalks and dirt fields of a sleeping world.

Now we know there is still a journey of discovery and relationship whereby we taste these "finished" realities. There are indeed times where it appears we go through the "fire" and emerge with a greater revelation of who we are and Whose we are. But we need to remember one important thing...

Fire does not create gold.

It reveals gold.

In reality, the gold is there all along, and many times there are certain trials that are not even necessary when we wake up to the fullness of who we are. Peter himself wrote to believers and discussed how they were going through trials, *if necessary* (see 1 Pet. 1:6). Trials only bring forth joy in our full redemption, and there is a place where "trials" even appear to dissipate. They may still exist, but we are walking over them in confidence instead of having them walk over us.

Like a Burning Torch

As the Lord begins to unveil more of how He sees the Shulammite, He then makes a promise to her. He says, "We will make you ornaments of gold and silver." Even though He already sees and declares the value that is in her, He promises to bring that beauty out into the light so that it adorns her life like shimmering jewelry (or fruit on a tree). This is a promise that will involve the work of the entire Godhead—the Father, Son, and Holy Spirit— for He says, *"We will make..."*

All of God is committed to seeing us walk out the fullness of our salvation. Let's take some seriously joyful comfort here. It is time to cease from laboring under our own wavering commitments to God and begin leaning upon God's commitment to us. Remember that the new covenant is a promise, not a contract. It is His perfect will and intention to present us blameless and complete before His presence. It is ultimately His faith in us that counts, not our own ability to conjure up faith ourselves. His faith is the solid bedrock by which we can move forward. This is a contradiction and offense to the religious mind, but a liberating truth that God's children need so desperately to hear.

So let's recap the beginning of the Shulammite's search for rest. The Lord calls her to remain teachable and humble. He calls her to honor the responsibilities He's given her, especially in the nurturing of those younger than her. He then begins to speak the truth of His love and the reality of her beauty. What He sees as clear as day He promises to bring out into the light that it might truly "adorn" her. He wants the whole world to see the glory she already possesses. It is similar to the words found in the book of Isaiah: "For Zion's sake I will not keep silent, and for Jerusalem's sake I will not keep quiet, until her righteousness goes forth like brightness, and her salvation like a torch that is burning" (Isa. 62:1).

Now He will take her to a very specific place where she can begin to step into these eternal truths. A place where all our roots must settle...

5 Coming to the Table Pt. 1

While the king was at his table,
My perfume gave forth its fragrance.

My beloved is to me a pouch of myrrh
Which lies all night between my breasts.

My beloved is to me a cluster of henna blossoms
In the vineyards of Engedi.
(1:12-14)

God, the Maker of all things, has heard the songful prayer of His beloved one. He has listened closely and has bent low to answer her longings for rest and for life. And now, having begun to speak of His love for her and the truth of how He sees her, He will bring her to the first real and tangible stop on her journey. This is a place known as the King's table. Up until now there has mainly been dialogue back and forth between the seeking Shulammite and her listening Lord. But a specific action takes place here. The Shulammite comes to Solomon's table, which of course is really the Lord's Table... the Table of the Lamb.

Solomon's father once sung of coming to a table as well. In that famous 23rd Psalm, David declared that God Himself prepared this table. And indeed, it was God and God alone who prepared the communion table—the table of the Lamb's sacrifice upon the cross. What's wonderful is that this *table* is one that is prepared in the presence of our enemies (Ps. 23:5). It is the gateway to victory and life. So just as He did with David, the Lord is bringing His searching Bride to this place as well.

It is no wonder that in the next line the woman says that her Beloved is like a "pouch of myrrh" lying over her heart. Myrrh was always associated with death since it was a spice used for preparing bodies for burial. It is therefore the sweet fragrance of the Lord's death that is resting over her heart. As she begins to eat at the Lord's Table, she begins to meditate upon the beauty and power found in the Lord's death on Calvary. This is the first real stop on the Bride's journey, and it is the first stop for any of us who desire to seriously grow in the paths of true life.

Greater than the Great Commandment

Many people will offer different "keys" and "steps" to find spiritual success. Reams and reams of books and conferences and media are put forth every day to try to capture the "way" to victory. But I tell you with every fiber of my being that there is only one true key to spiritual growth, life, and success—and that is to come and partake of the Lord's Table. To hold His death as myrrh over your heart and to let its fragrant truth rise into your nostrils and thus fill your mind with the smoke of His glory.

Many will tell you that if you want to find a deeper life in Christ, then you must do certain things. These "things" come in a wide array of explanations. Many of them are generic phrases that often leave people confused or feeling like the Most Holy Place is beyond their level of ability to suffer or be disciplined enough to enter. Though it's never said this way outwardly, these "things" give the impression that the veil is torn but you must still undergo great hurdles to somehow cross over into the Holy of Holies. Some of these hurdles will often be combined with biblical words like *surrender* or *sacrifice*. Sometimes the way into the

Holy of Holies is described as engaging in a life of fasting and prayer or deeper and more abandoned worship.

Now hear me clearly before you throw out this book. There are great treasures found within these disciplines and lifestyles. But what we need to know is that none of these things are the true access points to a fruitful spiritual life. They may aid part of the journey, but they are not the Lord's ultimate answer to the Shulammite's longing.

Why is this?

Because all those things ultimately point to what *we must do*, instead of what *He has done*. It leaves us with something to boast in. Yet at the end of the day we will all boast in one thing and one thing alone—and that is Jesus Christ and Him crucified (see 1 Cor. 1:27-2:2). Christianity is about His sacrifice more than our own sacrifice. Unfortunately, we have majored on the minors and minored on the majors in the church—and burnout, frustration, and disillusionment have often been the fruit.

I want you to notice that it is at the Table of the Lord where the Shulammite's fragrance is released: "While the king was at His table, my perfume gave forth its fragrance" (verse 12). Perfume and fragrance are powerful symbols of worship and prayer in the Bible. Our prayers are revealed as incense before the throne of heaven in Revelation 5:8, and it was an alabaster bottle of costly perfume that Mary of Bethany poured out in worship before Jesus. Our worship and prayers are a sweet-smelling aroma to the Lord.

So it was at the Table of the Lord that this beautiful fragrance was released. You see, a revelation of His sacrifice and *His work* will always lead to the sweetest kind of worship and prayer. But it is a worship and prayer of love, not of dry obedience to a commandment or some exalted lifestyle. The Lord's Table will also produce the most true and heartfelt surrender and sacrifice. Worship will come naturally when we realize the love God has for us. It is not really a discipline, but rather a spontaneous response that flows from a love relationship.

The foundational Scripture reference for this is the well-known verse, "We love, because He first loved us" (1 Jn. 4:19). Unfortunately, the emphasis in many well-intentioned messages has been, "We love, because we're commanded to." Or, "We love him, because it's the first and greatest commandment." And there has been much stress in the Body of Christ to put the first commandment first again. But did you know that there is something greater than the "first and greatest commandment?"

Remember that the first commandment is a *commandment*. It is part of *the law*. But it is actually God's love and His faithfulness to us that is even greater than our love and faithfulness to Him. So it is at the Table that we find a revelation of God's love for us. And because of that revelation, our own love, worship, and sacrifice will flow back to Him—and it is a flow that comes from a joyful heart, not from fear or a religious motivation.

This point cannot be overemphasized.

There are massive movements in the Body of Christ that have been putting *our* prayer and *our* worship as the foundation to revival (and the overall Eden life). There is a subtle, but dangerous element of religion in this, which ultimately brings the glory to us and puts the government on our shoulders instead of Christ's shoulders (see Isaiah 9:6). To be sure, this is not the intention of most leaders in these movements. Their hearts are sincere, but they are coming from an age-old emphasis on self-works (even "good" self-works like prayer), instead of focusing first and foremost on Christ's work at the cross.

Now of course these leaders would say, "We are promoting worship and prayer because it helps us look to God for His grace... They are avenues by which His grace flows." I completely understand this and would agree to a certain extent, but we must guard our hearts from the subtle emphasis on the self. If you were to study Paul's discipleship of believers and the epistles that were written to reinforce that discipleship, you will find him speak far more of Christ's nature and work than he ever speaks of spiritual disciplines. Re-read the letters sometime in their context and entirety—and let the Holy Spirit speak to you instead of solely filtering in the words of a book you've read or the words of the latest and hottest conference speaker. Read the epistles honestly. I believe that you will see that this is not some personal bias, but rather a true reading of the overarching themes and passions of the apostle's writings.

Do not be fooled by the subtle tweaking and softening of words that still carry the poison of religion and self-effort. Our worship and prayer are absolutely vital elements of the Kingdom, but they are not the foundation. There is only one foundation and that is Jesus Christ and His cross. Paul rarely talked about our spiritual works as the gateways to kingdom transformation. These are simply by-products—fruit—of a person coming alive to the sacrifice and love of Jesus. That will in turn lead to more and more fragrant worship and prayer (and thus abundant Kingdom transformation).

Please do not hear me speaking against such beautiful and powerful things as worship and prayer. This is really all about relationship with the Lord, and worship and prayer are natural parts of a real relationship with God. This is only meant to put first things first and to look honestly at how the King responds to the Shulammite's desires. There are many Shulammites today who are trying to find a fruitful life in Christ and they are often given nothing more than a discipleship program. But the King does not do that with His beloved. He leads her first and foremost to the place of His sacrifice and He calls her to hold this truth like myrrh over her heart.

In light of this, there is one more important note to add here. Many others will talk about a great move of "repentance" that needs to come to the world and that this will be the mark and beginning to true revival...

I agree. There is indeed a great repentance coming upon the Body of Christ.

However, it will be a "repentance" that is true to the original Greek word for repentance—*metanoia*. People think of repentance and they sometimes imagine people beating themselves up at the altar and wailing over their sins (again, putting the focus on us and our works). But the word *metanoia* actually means "a change of mind." Prophetic voices have accurately said that true repentance will be the catalyst for worldwide revival and harvest. But many have not realized this "repentance" will be a joyful change of mind about our identity and about the love of God, and the completed work of our High Priest and Lord. Yes, repentance and harvest is here and coming. But He will get the glory for it, not us. The capstone of church history will go on with shouts of only one word:

"Grace!" (see Zech. 4:7).

The Vineyards of Engedi

The part of the Song that surrounds the Lord's Table continues in the most vibrant way. The Shulammite begins to compare her Beloved to the henna blossoms found in the vineyards of Engedi. In the Passion Translation of the Song of Solomon, Brian Simmons points out that the word "Engedi" can actually be translated as "the fountain of the Lamb!"

The sweetest and most joyful fragrance emerges from the true revelation of Christ's work. Remember that the Shulammite is quite tired of her own deeds. She is looking for the righteousness and rest that no self-discipline or religious motivation can buy. So she is absolutely elated to find that the answer lies not in herself or in her own labors, but in the labors of the One who went before her, the Lamb of God. This is a sweet-smelling and joyful revelation to her heart, like henna blossoms in a glorious vineyard.

So let's turn to Paul's writings again. When the apostle to the Gentiles came to the young "Shulammites" in the Greek city of Corinth, he determined to focus his ministry on one thing alone—Christ and Him crucified (1 Cor. 2:2). So too, Jesus is coming to the entire Shulammite church and He is determined for her to know only one thing as well. On the journey to intimacy, love, and life, there is only one center and foundation. It is the One Thing needed, and that is the Word of Christ, the sacrificial Lamb of God.

The theme of the Song is beginning to emerge like morning dew covering the ground of its lyrics. This theme is the Person and work of Jesus. In fact, her coming to the Table only builds the opening notes to a clearer and more glorious melody in the pages to come. As said before, this is undoubtedly the Song of the Lamb as much as it is the Song of Solomon. The rest of this Song is actually an unfolding of Christ's love and sacrifice and what it all communicates to us as His purchased Bride.

There are great mysteries to this Song that will be unraveled in the chapters ahead, and the Bride will wrestle with much of it. So will you! But its fruit will be righteousness, peace, and joy in the Holy Spirit. We cannot emphasize enough that love and all other fruits of the Spirit will naturally emerge as we partake of the Lord's death and all that His death and resurrection entails.

Remember that it is the kiss of divine life for which she is searching. That divine life is the Holy Spirit who was first breathed into Adam. He is and always will be the true and satisfying "wine" of heaven. But the vineyards that hold that Wine find their placement and root system in one place alone...

The Fountain of the Lamb.

This is the place where God's perfect love was manifested.

6 Coming to the Table Pt. 2

Behold, you are fair, my love!
Behold, you are fair!
You have dove's eyes.

Behold, you are handsome, my beloved.
Yes, pleasant!
Also our bed is green.
The beams of our houses are cedar,
And our rafters of fir.
(1:15-17 NKJV)

As the first chapter of the Song draws to a close, there are some final things that emerge from the revelation and love flowing from the Lord's Table. We will look at them very briefly.

"How fair, how beautiful you are!" The Lord declares.

"How handsome you are!" The Shulammite responds.

When we look at this dialogue through the lens of the relationship between the Lord and the worshipper, it is astounding. The two are becoming lost in captivation of each other's beauty. This is worship in its deepest sense and the thought of it should cause our hearts to miss a few beats.

There is no greater worship but to be lost in God's beauty and glory. And yet worship only becomes more whole and complete when you look into His face and begin to see your own beauty and worth as well. It is beholding the Lord "as in a mirror," Paul says in his second letter to the Corinthians. As you declare His worthiness and glory, He begins to declare the glory that He has placed in you. This is because you are His true child, and you mirror His very being. The partaking of Christ's sacrifice (the food at the Table) always leads us to a deeper understanding of this, for in His sacrifice we drink of His redemption. As has been abundantly discussed, this food and drink then leads to heartfelt worship and prayer.

But what did Christ redeem? What is in that cup that we are called to drink from when we come to the Table?

Through His shed blood, the Lord redeemed us back to our original identity as the image-bearing children of God. He both revealed and restored our true value, which is one of the primary meanings of the word "redemption." That is why the worshipper calls him "handsome" and the Lord calls her "beautiful." It is the return to the mutual delight found between a father and son or a bridegroom and bride. To discover and embrace this brings a worship like no other. It will take a long time for the Bride to be established in this reality, but for now, she is drinking it in. The pure wine and milk of the Word is flowing to her heart and she will grow in her salvation as a result.

We must understand that this Song speaks to the relationship between the Lord God and the worshipper. It will help us see that true worship is the mutual delight that flows from a love relationship. We are not talking about an ancient pagan mindset of bowing low before a holy deity, while gravelling in fear and despising ourselves. The worship that surrounds the gods of Babylon and Egypt does not even come close to the worship of the One True God. This worship is the overflow of a relationship of intimacy where we find a reflected likeness in one another. There are certainly times of bowing low in silence as the terrifying beauty and awe of God consumes you. But this is the delightful fear of the Lord and not a slavish submission (see Isa. 11:3).

"Christianity is a relationship, not a religion" is a common tagline for many believers. Unfortunately, this phrase is often thrown around without us realizing its full power and implications. Christians all over the world will acknowledge that Christianity is a love relationship, but the reality of it goes way beyond what we have ever imagined. Let me try to explain this with an analogy...

Imagine a band of children from an extremely impoverished community who discover a shiny rock in the slums behind their homes. The kids who find this rock admire how different it is from the other rocks and go around showing it to other children, carrying it in their pockets and playing catch with it here and there along the way. But then imagine someone else comes along and takes a good look at that shiny rock and tells them they have discovered a 50-karat diamond! They knew it was cool and different and better than the other rocks in the lot (and they had told a lot of people about it as a result), but they had no clue that the value of this one "rock" could lift every single member of their community out of poverty and utterly change their lives forever. So too, the implications of the common phrase "relationship with God" go far beyond our current level of appreciation and understanding. We are often like children tossing around the truth that Christianity is special and separate from every other rock in the slum—but few have understood the full value of that truth and its life-changing implications upon our lives.

The Song of Solomon opens up the full picture of the phrase "relationship with God," like an infinitely wide-angle lens after we've been looking through a peashooter. The Song points us to the love relationship that defines true Christianity. We can even take out the word "Christianity" and simply call it *true Life*. It is a not a religion or a duty or a spiritual discipline. It is about a life lived where we are caught up into an intimacy with God that finds enjoyment and pleasure in one another. A life where we shout like the Shulammite in verse 16, "Yes, pleasant!" That word "pleasant" (*na'iym* in the Hebrew) can be translated as something pleasurable, lovely, absolutely delightful and sweet. Such is the fruit of worship and prayer that arises from a heart illuminated from the food and drink at our King's Table.

The Lord goes on from here to declare that she has dove's eyes. In this place of worship, the Lord is beginning to unravel more of how He sees her. The dove is always a symbol of the Holy Spirit in Scripture. We will discuss this element a little bit later in the Song, but for now we will simply say that Jesus sees His own Spirit's reflection in the eyes of His church.

But we all, with unveiled face, beholding as in a mirror the glory of the Lord, are being transformed into the same image from glory to glory, just as by the Spirit of the Lord.
(2 Cor. 3:18)

Our Resting Place

The Shulammite continues with a poetic description of her new surroundings. She first says that her "bed is green." Here we find that the Shepherd is leading her to the place of rest for which she sought in the beginning. The feast set before her has become "green pastures" for her soul. From here, she goes on to describe their "house." The table has expanded into green pastures, and in those pastures is a dwelling place...a home.

"The beams of our house are cedar, and are rafters are fir," she says. Now Solomon is not giving some bland architectural description in this passage. The Holy Spirit is moving upon him to write very specific words to describe this place. The table has transformed into a beautiful dwelling place made of specific elements.

Watchman Nee, in his beautiful commentary on the Song of Songs, points out something very interesting about these two elements of wood. He first explains that both kinds of wood were the main materials used in the construction of the temple. He then points out that "fir trees" in Solomon's day were products of a place called Death City and were commonly found growing in the graveyards near Judea. Once again, we see a hidden reference to death, which of course indicates the growing theme of the Song.

In Solomon's day, the temple was the place of God's real and manifest presence. As we see the likeness between the wood of her dwelling place and the wood of the temple, we find that she is in the place of God's presence. As she partakes of the bread and wine of redemption, her soul finds rest and this rest is rooted in the indwelling presence of Christ. Her awareness of His presence is growing and it is becoming a delightful place that she can call *home*.

Her covering, the rafters of the house, is the fir wood that speaks of death—Christ's death. She realizes that she is absolutely covered in mercy and grace. How can anyone embrace this level of worship and intimacy without first realizing the depths to which God went to demonstrate His love? The cross (that which the table speaks of) is how we see this most clearly. It is the place where God's unfathomable mercy towards us was displayed in its most bold form. There is no abiding enjoyment of God's presence without first realizing this.

Furthermore, how can somebody ever believe that the Lord reveals their true reflection without being "covered" in a revelation that their sins are completely gone? How can they taste such freedom without knowing the Lord no longer counts their sins against them? We are forgiven and clean, and this truth causes our souls to lie down in a "bed of green." This is the fountain that springs up with life and enables us to enjoy the manifest presence of God. The table has been set and the Shulammite is beginning to partake of its nourishing food.

Neverland

A final word...

In the early 1990s a new film rendition of the story of Peter Pan came out that met with great success. It was called "Hook" and was well-loved by moviegoers of all ages. It tells the story of Peter Pan who had left Neverland with Wendy and ended up growing up and having a family of his own. Along the way, however, Peter forgot who he was and got caught up in the burdens and busyness of adult life. He "lost the faith," so to speak, and fell from grace. He became a "mature adult" who was driven by intellect, reason and caution.

Through a series of different circumstances, Peter is brought back to Neverland and must learn to "wake up" to who he is in order to defeat Captain Hook, who has stolen his children. He must learn to fly. It's quite a beautiful analogy of the Gospel, as any good movie usually is. But what I want to share regarding this movie is one particular scene that marks the beginning of Peter's awakening. It all starts at a table.

After his unexpected arrival in Neverland, Peter sits down hungry for a meal with all the Lost Boys, who bring out tons of pots and dishes that are steaming hot. Peter sees the dishes and is excited to eat, but to his disappointment he finds that the dishes are all empty and the children are playing make-believe as they eat the food. So while all the children are eating from the empty dishes in their childlike faith, Peter idly and depressingly watches the plates pass him by. It takes an encounter with one of the kids that brings out elements of who he was in his past for him to wake up. At this moment, he suddenly and joyfully discovers the invisible food in the plates. He begins to *see* the meal set before him in the place of childlike faith. He then begins to feast upon it.

Coming to the Table of the Lord is quite similar. To many people, the table is only an empty ritual of bread and wine, which carries an empty message of something that happened 2000 years ago and has little relevance for today. At best, its message gives them some future hope of heaven one day, or a slight wink of mercy from a distant and holy God. Something that promises relationship, but is often nothing more than a Sunday encouragement. But there is so much more delicious food available at this table for those with eyes to see.

We are all called to partake. And this partaking includes an element of radical and childlike faith. It reminds us of who we truly are and it will ultimately empower us to take back those who are still in captivity! Many people have fallen from grace, and are now living in caution, reason, and busyness—burnt by the sun. But there is a table that sets us free from all of this. This is a table that is filled with fun and laughter as much as it is filled with new life and mercy. Some may idly let the plates pass by while others will dive in and eat of its nourishing food. But as we do eat, a catalyst builds. Something ignites. And soon, like Peter Pan (and the Shulammite much later in the Story), we learn to fly...

7 The Banner of Love

I am the rose of Sharon,
The lily of the valleys.

Like a lily among the thorns,
So is my darling among the maidens.

Like an apple tree among the trees of the forest,
So is my beloved among the young men.
In his shade I took great delight and sat down,
And his fruit was sweet to my taste.
He has brought me to his banquet hall,
And his banner over me is love.
(2:1-4)

I n the midst of the revelations pouring from the table and fountain of the Lamb, and the worship and prayer erupting in her heart, we find the Shulammite then giving an interesting description of herself. Some commentators have said that the Lord is speaking of Himself here, but it's quite clear from reading the context of the Bridegroom's reply in the next verse that it is still the Shulammite speaking when she declares that she is "the rose of Sharon" and the "lily of the valley."

Now there are many beautiful interpretations to this particular remark about the rose and the lily. The wonderful thing about the Scriptures is that they are multi-layered and one can draw a number of God-given conclusions from the text. There is not always a "right" answer in poetic Scriptures such as this. In my interpretation of the text, I am going to once again utilize a fact that Watchman Nee pointed out in his commentary on the Song. He explained that the "rose of Sharon" was actually a very common flower in the land of Sharon, which is a plain in Judea. Furthermore, the lilies found in the valleys of that region were also extremely common. Though they were beautiful, they were also superfluous.

From here we can see that the Shulammite is beginning to personally realize and admit her beauty when she compares herself to these types of roses and lilies. The last time she compared herself to something was the cracked tents of Kedar. This is a huge improvement! However, we will find that it is not as far as the Lord would have her go in her understanding of who she is. You can liken this to someone finally saying, "Yes, I know God loves me. He loves the whole world, so He must love me. For I am a lily in a sea of other beloved lilies..."

Now this is true. But there is incredible power of knowing God's personal love for you as an individual, not as just one lily in a field filled with many others. God doesn't love you because you are a part of the world. He loves you for you. There is incredible weight and glory found in this truth. An unbelievable shift happens in our hearts when we go from knowing the Lord died for the "world" to knowing He stretched out His arms and shed His blood for *me*. It's humbling and impactful and the person who has been touched by this reality does not look or act the same afterwards. Their life carries a different aura to it and a confident humility covers them like a cloak.

The Shulammite is gaining momentum, but is not completely there yet. The revelation that has come through the Lord's Table is certainly deepening her confidence in His love. But it has not been fully personalized yet. And so once more the Lord replies back to her with some amazing words. He acknowledges that she is a beautiful lily. But He separates her and brings her into the spotlight. "Like a lily among the thorns, so is my darling among the maidens!" She is uniquely special and stands apart. Her worth is not there because she is just one of many created things. Her worth is intrinsic to herself. God's love is not a nice general idea, but a very real and present reality.

In comparing other "maidens" to "thorns," this does not mean that God loves some people more than others. It is a comparison that He makes to us to let us know of our infinite uniqueness and beauty. That you, the individual, are *His favorite*. He may speak that to someone else, but it is no less true. There is enough room in the eternal heart of God for multitudes of favorites. Any earthly parent who has had more than one child can attest to this. There is a specialness to each child that does not diminish or generalize the love that a parent has for each of them.

The Rose of His Heart

Of course, there are other ways to unpack the beauty of what is being communicated in this portion of the text. The Passion Translation renders the Bride's words as, "I truly am the rose of His heart, the very theme of His song! I'm His ever-fresh lily growing even in the valley" (Sng. 2:1 TPT)! Such is the confidence that the Lord is awakening in His Bride.

Now whether it is a rose or lily, the comparison to a flower is breathtaking, especially when we understand its connection to us as people. Like a blossoming flower, the human soul is filled with layer upon layer of hidden beauty and aroma. The Shulammite is opening her heart to the Lord's love and sacrifice, and in doing so she is receiving the nourishment needed for her to "blossom." Even the most closed up person possesses an inner world of sheer delight to the heart of God. As one joins the journey of the Shulammite, the petals of our lives break and expand and the color that was always present shines forth. A fragrance emerges next, which is that life of heartfelt worship, love, and relationship.

The complete beauty that was there all along, of which the Lord had been constantly speaking, begins to emerge for all to see. While many other shepherds would grab onto the closed hearts of believers and try to pry open their petals with guilt and force, the Lord knows a much better way. "Do not awaken My love until she pleases," He will later say.

There is one more thing that needs to be added here before we move on. As already noted, the Lord uses a very important word to contrast the Shulammite's blossoming identity with the rest of the world. His use of the word "thorns" is a poignant and strategic metaphor. Beginning in Genesis 3, thorns and thistles relate directly to the curse. Here, the Lord is starting to unveil something much deeper about His sacrifice and its effect upon the Shulammite. She is a flourishing flower among a cursed world. He is starting to show her that the curse itself is not on her anymore and in fact can no longer touch her. This is part of Christ's sacrifice, in that He took the curse from us. The glory of this reality will be explored further on in the Song.

Christ redeemed us from the curse of the law, having become a curse for us (for it is written, "Cursed is everyone who hangs on a tree"). (Galatians 3:13)

The Apple Tree

With an overflowing heart, the Shulammite declares that her Shepherd and King is like an apple tree under which she has found the most pleasant shade. The myrrh, the Engedi vineyards, the bed of green, the dwelling place of His presence... Everything is building and multiplying from the simple revelation of the cross, the place of the Lord's Table. The searching Bride has found the tree of Calvary and is no longer just admiring it or talking about it—she is finally sitting under its shade. This is the tree that took away the curse of "thorns" and redeemed her life from the pit. It is a tree with fruit so powerful that when one eats it, it causes the darkened, Kedar self-image to slip away into a distant memory. It is the only place of true life and true rest.

The Shulammite has found a refuge that no work of her own hands could ever provide. Our own hands work so hard to provide shelter from the storms of accusation, fear, and doubt. We try and try and try, and this trying is probably what burnt out the Shulammite in the first place. She is now finding a place already prepared for her—a table, a house, a tree—that casts a canopy of protection and warmth over her soul. It has been built and planted by the hand of God alone.

There is such peace, such overwhelming joy that comes to our hearts when we begin to truly partake of our identity and the mysteries of our redemption in Christ—when we realize by trust that the curse is not on us and that sin is no longer a part of who we are. By faith—by eating and drinking of His Word—we encounter it in our own hearts and souls. Every curse, every voice of accusation, and every fear loses its sting under the shade of Christ's finished work. The Shulammite can feel this shade move over her heart and it brings a satisfaction like she has never experienced.

Bear in mind that her heart has met with great wounding over the years. Like an unrelenting sun beating upon her brow, the Shulammite has been hit over and over again by the judgments of others, by letdowns and disappointments, by her own failures, and by bitterness, fear, and turmoil. And now, her raw and weary heart has been bathed and dipped in the most refreshing water to ever spring forth from the ground. This is the water of life, which is free to all and brings complete and total refreshment.

The House of Wine

It also brings complete and total intoxication...

The Shulammite builds upon her poetic utterances with an expression that many English translators call "the banquet hall." This, however, is a very poor translation of the original Hebrew wording. In fact, most English translations recognize this and will mark the literal meaning as a footnote in the text. The Scriptures are actually saying that the King has brought her into His "House of Wine!"

The metaphors keep rolling in, and this one carries great significance as well. Wine has come up a few times throughout the Song and it's something that shows up quite often throughout the rest of the Scriptures. Jesus Himself uses wine to symbolize the most precious thing in the universe as well as the central theme of His Word: the shed blood of His new covenant. Now it is interesting that Jesus uses wine as a symbol for something such as this. I assure you, He makes this connection not just because the color of wine is similar to blood, but for many other reasons as well...

Wine, according to King David, "gladdens the heart of man" (Psalm 104:15). Wine is known to ease the heart, lifting sorrows and removing inhibitions. Of course, we know that other Scriptures point out that too much wine leads to the destruction. Nonetheless, there is a spiritual connection here revealing that the Lord's covenant has an effect upon the heart similar to natural wine. When one drinks in the love of God and truly sits under the apple tree of the cross, there is an intoxication of the soul that is overcome by peace, joy, and laughter. Inhibitions are also removed. Like Peter coming out of the upper-room and boldly preaching to a crowd he had just been hiding from (and to whom he had denied the Lord), there is an uninhibited strength that comes when one emerges from drinking the "new wine" of the new covenant.

In the Song of Songs, the Bride has not been led into a place of regulated wine-tasting and small sipping. Rather she has been led into the very *House of Wine* where the drinks are overflowing and the King has plenty of back-ups in case any bottles run dry. She is brought into a kingly banquet where there is an abundance of spiritual meat and emboldening drink. This is a feast that never runs dry. Such is the inheritance of the saints and the bounty won at the cross. Everyone who is thirsty and everyone who is hungry is invited to eat and drink and to never hunger or thirst again. This is the place the Shulammite has been discovering, or perhaps re-discovering.

The Theme of it All

Everything she has come across in the beginning of her journey begins to billow up in her heart, and with a mighty shout she releases another metaphor and lyric that sums up everything said so far. In the midst of her intoxication, the Bride begins to realize something. Something that has the potential to quell every future doubt and fear. She begins to realize what is causing this shade in the first place—a shade that brings sheer delight and reveals an endless banquet of righteousness, joy and peace.

With simplicity and clarity, the Shulammite declares, "His banner over me is love!"

To understand the magnitude of this statement, we may need to explain a little bit about the use of banners in Solomon's day. These were not just nicely embroidered cloth hanging around birthday parties or fellowship halls. Back then, banners carried extreme significance in a time when local stores couldn't just print off whatever message a person wanted to display. Banners took a lot of time, money and skill to create and they carried several key purposes.

One purpose of the banner was to put forth in writing an official edict or proclamation by the King so that all could see it and remember it. They would be hung at the entranceway of a city or on the wall of a great castle facing the direction of the people. If a new and important law was put into effect, a banner would be hung in this way so that it was known to all the people of the kingdom. Jesus hanging from the cross is the standard and banner that declares the proclamation of God's righteousness and grace to humanity.

Banners were also used in war during Solomon's era (and of course long before then as banners have always been a special form of communication amongst the cultures of the world). Exhibiting a crest or symbol, a banner would clearly declare the identity of the army. It would then be used as a rallying point for troops to gather and fight in unity. After a battle was won, a banner would then be firmly planted in the ground to declare the king's possession of new territory.

So let's take these things together in light of the simple statement, "His banner over me is love." First of all, love is the official proclamation and edict of God over our lives—one that He would have us remember and remember well. It is also our rallying point and the only place where we find true unity with God (and thus with one another). When we feel scattered, defeated and burdened with unending issues that blur our vision, the love of God is always the dawning light that brings us into a place of stability and renewal. To disbelieve or forget the love of God is to lose a battle that has already been won.

Furthermore, God Himself is love. Love is therefore the crest and symbol of all that He is. It is the fabric of His very being. Love is not just an attribute that the Lord has when He is in a good mood or when we are doing well. It is the center and source of His own identity and every one of His actions moves by its outworking essence, like dials spinning on a clock's wheel. He planted the very banner of His being over our hearts, having overcome the territory of our lives by love alone. There is no hidden motive or agenda in His pursuit of us. We are the Lord's possession and inheritance and it is His other-giving, selfless, and infinite lovingkindness that has won us over. The very theme and message of our life is now the love of God.

When people study literature and try to extrapolate the full meaning of a certain text, they will often first try to discover hidden themes within it. Finding the themes and underlying messages brings a sense of completion and understanding in studying a piece of writing. Moreover, people all over the world and throughout the millennia have been searching for a theme and message to the larger world around them. It is the continual pursuit of the meaning of life. But the Shulammite has found this theme, and more importantly, its source. It is the love of God—and love towards one another—that is the theme and banner of life. Everything makes sense when we come to see this like the Shulammite.

There are many other "banners" being heralded these days over the Body of Christ. People emphasize many different things and it can make our journey somewhat complicated at times. If certain ministries were to have a flag symbolizing their focus, you might see some flags wearing the banner of spiritual warfare, some of the end-times, some of discipleship or church-planting. But the Shulammite has found joy in what everything is centered in.

A moment of clarity has come to her in the House of Wine that outshines and simplifies everything else. The poetic symbols of cedar and apples, wine and myrrh all melt away for a moment as the victorious theme of it all comes into light. Like a woman dancing in a room of shadows filled with familiar yet unclear shapes, a light switch is thrown on and everything is made visible. Ancient and joyful understanding arrives at her consciousness like an eagle coming back to its nest. All is known and all is well in this place. Everything else will fade away, but the truth of this banner will abide forever.

The overarching theme and message God is speaking over us is love. That is what this story is all about, and that's what life itself is all about. It is the melody playing all throughout the universe, and it is the sons and daughters of God who are called to wake up and begin singing its tune. As this happens, we will call all of creation (even those still wrapped up in thorns) to see this banner and dance under its shade as well.

First Selah

I would like to stop for a moment and attempt to explain how life-changing a simple "pause" can be. A pause, or *Selah* as David called it in the songs that he composed, could bring immeasurable change to the heart and soul.

Let's say a man goes on vacation and spends every day walking past a beautiful lake. He admires its beauty, but quickly walks past it to take care of other things on the week's agenda. But let's imagine that in the edges of the lake's shifting water lies a priceless golden watch. This watch, however, could only be seen if one looks carefully enough and pauses long enough for the light of the sun to hit the water in such a way that a reflection is cast by the gold underneath. If our vacationer did not pause long enough to look at the water and then see the treasure within, he could have missed possessing something of incredible value. Something that he could have taken back home after the vacation was over.

So you too, reader, are on a vacation in reading this book (or any other book for that matter). A vacation is nice in that it takes you away for a brief period of time. However, I am far more interested in you taking away something that benefits and impacts your entire life (especially the day to day grind where vacation lakes and majestic theology seem thousands of miles away).

And so I would encourage you to truly pause and reflect as you continue through this book. It might require more time and more patience, but I believe as you do you will find the sun catching the waves of your heart at the right moment, where things begin to "click" and a treasure of inestimable value is brought into your possession. Take time to meditate and chew on these realities. Re-read portions that strike your heart in a particular way, whether bringing joy and peace or even challenge and offense.

The Holy Spirit whispers in our hearts, and the heart's movements can be quite subtle at times. Do not be rushed in moving along. Enjoy the view and trust in the ability of the sun to reveal things that lie below the water...

8 Still Asleep

Sustain me with cakes of raisins,
Refresh me with apples,
For I am lovesick.

Let his left hand be under my head
And his right hand embrace me.

I charge you, O daughters of Jerusalem,
By the gazelles or by the does of the field,
That you do not arouse or awaken my love
Until she pleases.
(2:5-7)

The first portion of the Song has reached a dramatic climax. The Shulammite is overcome by everything she has seen and tasted. The King James Version says that she is now "sick of love" (*sick* in the sense of being weak or fainting), which is actually a better translation than "lovesick." The Hebrew signifies that she is overflowing with love and thus made weak to the point of fainting. This is why she asks in the fifth verse to be refreshed and strengthened, that she might stand up under the weight of this glory. She desires to continue to live in this reality, but is unable to do so at the moment. She feels herself unable to handle or "sustain" the truths that have been set before her.

So it is here that she longs for union—for a permanent stay in the King's palace, not just a nice visit during a time of worship and meditation, which is what most of this has been so far. The phrase, "Let his left hand be under my head and his right hand embrace me" is a sexual reference. There is no way around it. A man's left hand is not under a woman's head unless she is lying down. The right hand then embracing her needs no further explanation if you understand the first part. Now, as we said in the beginning, the reality of sex is but a signpost to something greater and more tangible. It speaks of two becoming one. It speaks of the permanent union she now desires between her and God. But it is at this point that a new melody and different lyrics begin to take shape. The Lord will begin to challenge the Shulammite's perceptions and even her very prayer. He will soon show her the reality that she already has the union she craves...

At this point in the story, we will find that the Shulammite is still spiritually asleep. Though there was improvement from comparing herself to the "tents of Kedar" to the "rose of Sharon," she is not yet at the place of being fully awake to the Lord's words. She has experienced wonderful things in His presence, but now she feels herself leaving the weight and reality of it. She feels she cannot handle it and wants something to sustain her. And it is here that we find the words, *"Do not awaken my love until she pleases."*

Many translations will say, "Do not awaken love until *it* pleases." This lends itself to the interpretation that this Scripture signifies the importance of waiting until the right time for marriage and sex. If you have come this far in the book, I pray that your eyes have seen enough of the land of this Song to know that its terrain covers much more than earthly marriage. The King will often refer to the Shulammite as "My love" (such as when He later says, "Arise, My love") and so here He is surely speaking to the daughters of Jerusalem about *His love*, the Shulammite. She is the one who is still asleep.

Now she has certainly come a long way. She has begun to taste and see that the Lord is good. Like a newborn babe, she has drunk of the milk of the good Word of God. The Word that declares our redemption through the work of Christ. She has come to His table, sat under His tree, and dined in the House of Wine where her heart finally caught a vision of the banner that defines it all. This is the banner that reveals the essence of God, the very love that provides the spin to all the infinite clockwork of His being. That golden watch lying in the waters of His Word.

Yet in spite of her encounters with the Lord and the revelation that has been hitting her, everything becomes too much for her and she begins to faint back into sleep. Hence, she desires to stay permanently in the house through the reality of union (*...let his left hand be under my head*). It is one thing to have an encounter with God and His truth, but it is another to live life in the sustained enjoyment and awareness of it all. The Shulammite now desires to continue to soak and bake in the pure sunlight of Christ, like grapes before they become "raisins." So she asks for the "apples" of the tree (the cross) to awaken her heart again, and the sun-kissed raisins to invigorate her back into the place of peace. These elements reveal her desire for something to strengthen her that she might permanently abide in the place of intimacy and love that she has begun to experience.

Put into other words, the Shulammite feels that she is losing her grasp on the wonderful truths being shown to her. She has found herself unable to stand up in the House of Wine. This is much like when a baby learns to stand up for the first time, when their knees and muscles are not yet at the point where standing is an easy and natural thing. The Shulammite is unable to stand up permanently. There have been moments of arising, but now she feels herself falling back and unable to remain in the revelation of perfect love and peace.

This is a common experience for all of us in our journey of knowing and encountering God. For those that want to move beyond "church-ianity" and burn-out into a place of rest, righteousness, and life, there is always the starting place of the table, where if we allow the truths of the cross to penetrate our hearts we can experience incredible depths of peace. However, there comes a point where that peace and grace begins to challenge deep-rooted thinking within us, and this often causes us to stumble in our walk forward as we hold on to old ways of thinking. We might slip up and forget who we are, and are then tempted in that moment to doubt the truths of the table and the tree. As a result, we begin to go back to self-effort or condemnation. We took baby steps into the truth, but found ourselves falling back into old fears in the face of opposition or contradiction to God's intoxicating message. We then long for the raisins and apples of His revelation to come and catapult us back into the place of peace.

Many have had the experience of reading a book, attending a conference, or entering into a time of worship and prayer where a certain revelation penetrates our hearts and we feel absolutely on top of the world. That is because we *are* on top of the world, since we are catching glimpses of our present co-seating with Christ (see Eph. 2). Yet when we come out of those specific set-apart times, we often find that the realities appear to fade as we begin to judge our lives by our emotions or other seeming contradictions to the Word. This all has to do with an issue of sleepiness still pervading our lives that keeps us from being fully awake to the glories of the cross and the full love of God.

As we come to the next portion of the Song, it will become even clearer that the Shulammite has not fully awakened yet to the Lord's love and to the truth of who she is. Though she may not realize it right away, she is still somewhat under the groggy stupor of religion and fear. Through her communion with the Lord, His love and His Word have been planted like a seed in her heart. But that seed will now be called forth into its unavoidable blossoming. So it is with us as well.

Thankfully, we will find great encouragement and comfort in the Lord's exposing of the Shulammite's sleep. He does not scream in her ear for her to wake up and get her act together and start walking on her own two feet. "Until she pleases" speaks to the fact that He wants her to grow in and through *grace*. It must be real and of the heart. It must be of her own inner desire and the natural birthing of Christ within her. The lily's petals cannot be pried open out of season. This is something that many shepherds of struggling flocks fail to comprehend. Babies cannot be forced to walk. Time, mercy and care are all parts of the process. This is not to advocate the avoidance of "tough love" or speaking the truth plainly to people. Some people are so spiritually asleep that it's killing them and we need to go to extreme measures to get them to see the futility of their actions (see Jude 1:23).

Nonetheless, I believe the Lord knows the consequences of allowing slumber and blindness to consume our lives. He knows that these things have a way of "disciplining" us in and of themselves. He does not come as one who adds to that discipline with condemnation or harshness. He knows we need the voice of a Good Father and a Good Shepherd to bring encouragement and grace in the midst of our self-defeating slumber. This is the true voice of the Lord.

In the next part of the Song we will enter into the Bride's sleep. The Lord does not want others to force her out of it in an untimely or ungracious way. Instead, He Himself will enter into her dream world and will call her out of it through a deepening revelation of the truths she has already begun to taste.

He will call her to rise up and stand.

9 Arise, My Love

Listen!
My beloved!
Behold, he is coming,
Climbing on the mountains,
Leaping on the hills!
My beloved is like a gazelle or a young stag.
Behold, he is standing behind our wall,
He is looking through the windows,
He is peering through the lattice.
(2:8-9)

So we have come to see that the Shulammite is still asleep. The wine has been uncorked and the aroma has flooded her senses, stirring her in her bed and leaving her unsatisfied with anything less than the intimacy and rest she had temporarily encountered. But there is so much more in the bottle for her to now drink. In uncorking the wine, she has begun to smell a fresh revelation and has come in touch with a higher wisdom and perspective. But now the revelation must translate into consistent experience. This is what the Lord is calling her into as the Song deepens. The wine has an effect that will transform everything about her life, but is she willing to drink it to the point of encountering its effect? Being intoxicated on the wine of the Gospel leads to something. It looks like something.

In this portion of the Song we find an issue of an alleged separation and distance between the Bride and the Bridegroom. Now I use the word *alleged* because we know from the myrrh, the fountain of the Lamb, and many other symbols sung out so far, that she has already been united to Christ through His death. He will never leave her nor will He ever forsake her. This is one of the main things that the Lord's Table communicated. There is no getting away from this truth no matter how well a man may preach it and make union with God seem like a far off reality.

But the one who joins himself to the Lord is one spirit with Him.
(1 Cor. 6:17)

...lo, I am with you always, even to the end of the age.
(Mat. 28:20)

The Shulammite, however, is not understanding this. There is still a lie being played out. A lie of distance and separation. And this lie will reveal the very center and source of her sleepiness and exhaustion. In fact, this lie will reveal the source of all our sleepiness and that which keeps us from living in the complete revelation of the cross. So like a skillful surgeon, our Great Physician is going to the root issues that keep the Shulammite from experiencing the Eden life that she longs for.

We find here that something—some "wall"—is separating them. The Shulammite is behind this wall and the Bridegroom is on the other side calling her to come out. This is a wall, we shall see, that exists only in the mind. For she is one with Him in His victory over sin. He is her righteousness and her life. Indeed, she is hidden within Him. And yet there is a wall keeping her from encountering this, which is perhaps why the apostles encouraged us to "be renewed in the spirit of your mind" (Eph. 4:23).

The phrase "behind our wall" refers to the wall that all the daughters of Jerusalem have held up, for she says *our wall*. This is indeed the "dividing wall" that Paul speaks of in his letter to the

Ephesians. It is actually the wall of the *law*. This is because the law communicates enmity between God and us and also speaks of a big thick veil that separates us from the Holy of Holies—from His presence, from His love, and from the permanent, abiding shade of the Apple Tree. Look closely at the following verses:

> *But now in Christ Jesus you who formerly were far off have been brought near by the blood of Christ. For He Himself is our peace, who made both groups into one and broke down the barrier of the dividing wall, by abolishing in His flesh the enmity, which is the Law of commandments contained in ordinances...*
> *(Eph. 2:13-15)*

> *But their minds were hardened; for until this very day at the reading of the old covenant the same veil remains unlifted, because it is removed in Christ. But to this day whenever Moses is read, a veil lies over their heart.*
> *(2 Cor. 3:14-15)*

To this day, the same wall remains a great issue in the church and lies like dry rot under the wooden framework of our theologies and ministries. Though we may not sacrifice bulls or religiously keep away from pork, the striving and separating elements of the law still pervade many of our pulpits and airwaves. It is indeed one of the main things keeping the church asleep and unaware of the full glories of her salvation. It keeps back the flood of the Spirit from bubbling up out of us and it keeps us from the radical love that Jesus said would transform the world. In other words, it keeps back the full inebriation of the wine (which, in more biblical terms, is "the fruit of the Spirit").

This wall inhibits us in two ways. First, it communicates a sense of contention (enmity) between God and us. Now this may only be a minor sense of contention. Again, we may come to understand and even say out loud "God loves me." But sometimes hidden underneath those words are sneaking suspicions that He is still holding something against us, especially in regards to our present and future sins and weaknesses. A sin or guilt consciousness is still allowed entrance into our hearts, and this guilt immediately puts a stop to love's shade. In the words of the apostle Peter, we become "short-sighted" and forget that we were cleansed from our sins (see 2 Pet. 1:9).

Secondly, this wall causes us to see the life of Christ as something to be attained and sought after by our own efforts. This ultimately leaves us with a greater sense of shame when we look at ourselves and feel that we fall short of the glory of Jesus. Or, it leads to a convenient change in our doctrines, relegating victory and "greater works" to life after death or at least after years and years of striving and suffering. It sees Jesus way out "over there" climbing on the mountains of difficulty with ease while we are "over here" in our little walled-in house of "lesser works." Jesus is "leaping on the hills" while we are in a *separate* place, far from that glorious life.

All of this shows that the Shulammite does not yet see herself *in Christ*. She does not understand that the Father embraces her as He would Jesus Christ Himself—that there is not the slightest hint of blame or condemnation in the Father's heart towards her. Moreover, she does not realize that she is united to Christ in all of His mountain-leaping nature. While starting to understand His love, she does not fully comprehend who she is in her union with Him. So we find that she is still asking for union ("let his left hand be under my head...") while not seeing that she already has it.

So to the Shulammite in this Song—and to the church today—Jesus has some powerful words in response to this alleged separation. Words of incredible truth and hope. Her beloved "responds" and speaks to her through the veil over her heart. His words come from another dimension, a completely different perspective than the earthly systems of man and his religions. Jesus's words are spirit, and they are life. They are truer than our earthly experiences and louder than the voices of condemnation and fear.

He says to her...

> *Arise, my darling, my beautiful one,*
> *And come along.*
> *For behold, the winter is past,*
> *The rain is over and gone.*
> *The flowers have already appeared in the land;*
> *The time has arrived for pruning the vines,*
> *And the voice of the turtledove has been heard in our land.*
> *The fig tree has ripened its figs,*
> *And the vines in blossom have given forth their fragrance.*
> *Arise, my darling, my beautiful one,*
> *And come along!*
> *(2:10-13)*

The Lord bypasses her veiled, self-focused perceptions and speaks with heavenly clarity. It is here that our King will begin to more fully articulate the reality of the new creation and the truth of what He has accomplished on the cross. One cannot read these words without making reference to the words of the apostle:

> *Therefore if anyone is in Christ, he is a new creature; the old things passed away; behold, new things have come. Now all these things are from God, who reconciled us to Himself through Christ and gave us the ministry of reconciliation, namely, that God was in Christ reconciling the world to Himself, not counting their tres-*
> *passes against them...*
> *(2 Cor. 5:17-19)*

She may have begun to taste some glorious things at the Table, but now she is called to feast on all that it provides. Like the lead character Neo in the movie *The Matrix*, the Shulammite is being invited to take the red pill and see how far down the rabbit hole of redemption goes. She has begun to understand the love and grace associated with the cross, but now the Lord is calling her to see the new world and the new life that the cross has opened up.

The winter and the rain speak of an old season for humanity. The winter communicates a time when fruit and blossoms are not able to come forth because they are covered in snow and ice. Spiritually, this speaks of an age when man could not bear the fruit of the divine nature and blossom into our original design as the image-bearers of God. All they could do was live by the righteousness of the law, trying to live the right way by our own self-effort. But there is no organic life there. All that can be produced is what the flesh can muster up. When I say "flesh," I am referring to the animate human frame disconnected from the life of God and veiled from its true identity in Him.

Rain is mentioned next in the Bridegroom's words. This speaks of the judgment that comes upon man's wintry ways. While rain is typically a positive symbol throughout the Scriptures, there is a flipside to its symbolism as well. In the negative sense, rain is associated with the judging floodwaters of Noah. It speaks to the destruction that erupts from our sin—the unfruitful life of humanity frozen under the ice of a false identity and stemming from the Tree of the Knowledge of Good and Evil. The rain communicates a hostility between God and man, which ends up manifesting itself in destruction and barrenness.

Mankind was given a "wall" of protection in order to guard us from the rain of destruction that follows our wintry ways. This wall of the law was meant to provide a legal barrier to keep us from the devastation of the rain. If we obey its commands, then blessing and fruitfulness will come upon our lives and we can start to get a taste of Eden again. But if we do not follow the full code of the law, then a curse manifests itself in our lives and we find ourselves burning under the heat of its rays.

Of course, we know that the law did not bring true protection. It served a different purpose that the Shulammite has not fully understood. Paul calls the law a tutor that led us to Christ (see Gal. 3-4). It gives us a glimpse of what righteousness looks like, but ultimately reveals our need for a Savior to bring us into that place of righteousness. Like Moses, who was not allowed to enter the Promised Land but was still given a glimpse of it, the law gives us a picture of righteousness (the Eden life), but does not let us enter in (see Deut. 3:23-28).

Now the law may allow us temporary moments of relief depending on how disciplined we are and how much willpower we can muster up to obey its commands. This is why some people have a hard time coming out of a legal mindset, because they have a decent amount of strength to live under its false protection. Though they do not experience a true rest in the Father's embrace, they think that periods of blessing under the law constitute a sufficient life. But even after the golden periods in our lives (like the golden periods of Israel's history), the fruit of the law still comes forth and we enter into a cycle of sin-repentance-sin and wilderness spirituality. The life of Christ is mostly far out in the distance while we lick our wounds and pray that God would rend the heavens and deliver us (not believing that He already has in Christ!).

There is no true intimacy and rest behind the wall. It is a dark and cold shade that is nothing like the shade found under the apple tree of the cross—the Tree of Life. It is all about a legal relationship that keeps a safe distance between the Lord and us. It is in fact an extension of mankind's decision to eat from the Tree of Good and Evil (Right and Wrong). The law was meant to show us the futility of living outside of union with God, who is the tree and source of true life. It led to nothing but robotic duty and loveless obedience instead of abiding and resting in the fact that we are naturally the holy image-bearers of the Father.

Ultimately, life behind the wall is one where we see ourselves as slaves and not sons. Servants, but not friends. A concubine, but not a beloved Bride. So let's bring this all back to the Shulammite. The Shulammite is being shown that she is still in a legal relationship with God, which is based more out of fear than confidence. There is still something in her thinking that fears the rains of His judgment. Furthermore, there is a lack of confidence in her ability to live a holy and fruitful life. This is because living behind the wall also means trying to bear fruit by one's own effort, instead of resting and trusting in the springtime air of the Spirit to bring forth that fruit. Perhaps this is part of the reason she fell out of the place of grace in the first place when she recognized her need for something to "sustain" her.

The banner of God's love had confronted her with realities behind her imagination, but this section makes it apparent that the old ways of the law are still creeping into her mind. Even in understanding the basics of grace, love, and the work of the cross, we still find here a clinging to the old. The Shulammite is embracing God's love and acceptance with one hand, while holding to the wall with the other. And so the wall continues to call to her, saying that the banner is too good to be true. *There has got to be a catch somewhere (and you better watch out that you don't go too far into this message of grace and union).*

This life of law—one of fear, slavery, self-effort and a perceived separation between her and Jesus—this is the life from which the Shepherd will now call her to come away.

Come Away, My Beloved!

And Christ will come like a Lion and a Lamb. A fierce and kind King who, with a merciful roar, will make His plea and declaration to His church:

The winter and the rain are over and gone! That season has come to end, My beloved one... Come away from the law, from your self-protection and your fear. Come away from a life of self-effort, where you still see yourself separated from who I am in all My fullness. A life that does not believe you are just as holy and just as beloved to the Father as I am! A life that still fears the rain of punishment and the winter of powerlessness. Be free of that lie...

Such is the accomplishment of the cross, which forever tore down the dividing wall and brought us into union with Christ.

Jesus came and revealed that God is for us, and that His love was upon us, even when we lived as enemies. He revealed the true face of God, which was always shining forth with mercy, forgiveness and peace. He atoned for the sins of the world and restored our identity as the children of a holy and infinite God. There is no more need to strive or try to live by the righteousness of the law. Now we live in a righteousness of trust—a life that believes that we are one with Him, already made righteous through His work on the cross. It is not about "doing" but "being." Any *doing* simply flows out of that place of trust and being.

The Shulammite is most likely staying behind her wall because she believes the winter and the rain is still out there somewhere. She fears a life of true freedom and grace, because she does not yet trust in the fullness of her redemption. She has heard the Word, she has smelled the aroma, but she has not yet let it settle into a place of trust within her heart.

But the rain is truly gone. There is no more wrath upon her. There is no more fear in the light of God's true face and love. There needn't be anymore worry of hell or even a fear of what failure may bring in this present life. There is only a love-relationship to be embraced if she will just let go of her self-protecting wall and the religious systems that man has set up—systems where we argue and worry about how to legally attain or keep our salvation. As though our salvation is ultimately dependent upon us and not on the Lord...as though the Lord is always one step away from throwing us into excruciating and eternal pain, and is holding back on this as long we keep to a certain standard. It is very hard to trust in His abiding love in the midst of such legal and fear-based mindsets. But there is no more need to worry about somehow pleasing God enough to keep back the curse and destruction. These are all mindsets that arise from a veiled heart that is still flooded with condemnation. One that has not seen the true face of the Father and the sufficiency of His Son's blood.

There is a new reality inaugurated through the death, burial and resurrection of Christ. A new world has opened up. The winter of law, sin and death is past and the springtime of resurrection and grace has dawned. The King is now announcing the fullness of the Gospel to the hiding Shulammite. Next, He will strengthen His point further by showing her the tangible signs that prove this "New Thing" of His resurrection has come...

> *Do not call to mind the former things,*
> *Or ponder things of the past.*
> *Behold, I will do something new,*
> *Now it will spring forth;*
> *Will you not be aware of it?*
> *I will even make a roadway in the wilderness,*
> *Rivers in the desert.*
> *(Isaiah 43:18-19)*

The Signs of Times...

In the Song of Songs, Christ declares several signs of the new "springtime" to help His beloved one see that it is indeed the season of a new world and a new Kingdom of peace and reconciliation. He starts by mentioning the blossoming of flowers in the land, which is obviously a reminder of physical springtime and new life. In this sense, however, it is a reminder of the season of Christ's physical resurrection. In helping both the Shulammite and us trust in this message of grace, Jesus is first pointing to His own physical resurrection from the dead.

Christ is called the "first-fruits" of a worldwide resurrection (see 1 Cor. 15:20). His resurrection is the chief and primary sign that the "New Thing" has arrived and we can come away from the old and move into a new creation life of peace with God. Christ's resurrection is the first sign of the Kingdom's inauguration, even if it is not fully revealed in all the earth yet. This is because His resurrection is also the revealing of our own resurrection. We are fully included in all that His resurrection entails. Let's look closely at the words of the prophet Hosea:

> *He will revive **us** after two days;*
> *He will raise **us** up on the third day,*
> *That we may live before Him.*
> *(Hos. 6:2)*

The great mystery of Christ's work is that we were included in it. He is the High Priest and Representative for all humanity. He came and lived not only for us, but *as us*. He obeyed and fulfilled the law for us, and now we are called to effortlessly eat of the fruit of His harvest and victory. Hence, all glorying and boasting is in Him alone. When He died, we died. Our sinfulness—Adam and his whole race—died in that crucifixion. And when He was raised, we were all raised to new life as well. Jesus entered into Adam's wintry mess and took all the floodwaters of judgment upon Himself. This was a finished work that brought complete righteousness to us just as Adam's work brought complete condemnation.

The winter is past. The rain is over and gone. We are now hidden in Christ, who is our righteousness, sanctification, and redemption.

We may now *come away* and "live before him" because we are accepted and included in the Beloved, Jesus Christ. This is a mystery that the Holy Spirit longs to reveal more fully to the church, which is comprised of those who have believed and received this message. It is this truth that the Song is whispering through its melody to those still asleep.

He goes on from here to speak of the turtledove's activity, which symbolizes the Holy Spirit's new activity throughout the earth. The presence of the Holy Spirit among men, which started in Judea and has now begun to reach the ends of the earth, is the next sign of this new season. The Spirit's presence upon Jew and Gentile after the physical resurrection of Jesus is something we should look to in order to trust this amazing message of new-ness and grace. Vines in blossom also speak to the presence of His Spirit on the earth. The very presence of the Spirit within us is proof that God is with us and the age of separation is now over. This is the new wine that is ready to be drunk so that the fruit of the Spirit (not the false fruit of the law) can come forth in the land.

Jesus is speaking to the sleeping church (much like the apos-tles did to the sleeping nation of Israel after Jesus ascended to heaven) and telling us to observe the signs all around: "*It's already here!*" He shouts. "*Don't you see? Rise up, and come out of the illu-sion of separation and hostility. Your guilt and your sin has been removed as far as the east is from the west. You are in me and I am in you. Wake up...and believe!*"

Jesus's resurrection is far more than a one-time event to cele-brate once a year, or even once a week. It is a declaration of the end of all death and sin and the beginning of "one new man" coming forth on the earth (revisit Ephesians 2). The old man, Adam, has been crucified (Rom. 6:6). The winter of Adam's false identity and the rain of judgment that came upon it is over, for Christ has taken it all upon Himself. God is no longer counting men's sins against them.

For this is like the days of Noah to Me when I swore that the waters of Noah would not flood the earth again. So I have sworn that I will not be angry with you nor will I rebuke you.

For the mountains may be removed and the hills may shake, but My lovingkindnes will not be removed from you, and My covenant of peace will not be shaken," says the Lord who has compassion on you.
(Isa. 54:9-10)

The advancing church is comprised of those who truly believe the above Scripture. I encourage you to read it again and remember that it applies to the present covenant that we are already in. The advancing church, filled with the truth of that Scripture, no longer identifies itself with Adam and the old era of hostility and contention. Instead, we see ourselves fully included in the New Man and believe in a new season of complete peace and victory with God. Furthermore, we believe we are co-resurrected with Christ. As a result, "The darkness is passing away and the true light is already shining," (1 Jn. 2:8). The church is made up of those who radiate this new light to a world that is still completely asleep. We are the sons and daughters of the day, calling the rest of the earth into a new dawn as well.

The Song and Church History

We have looked at a lot of different Scriptures in this chapter. The purpose of these verses is to tie the Beloved's poetic words into the overall theme and hope of the Gospel. Through our union with Christ, we are now equipped with all we need to scale the mountains of injustice and sin. Nevertheless, fear and deception can often hold us back from this, even though the victory has already been accomplished. The Shulammite tasted wondrous things in the House of Wine, but we find that a legal, law-based mindset is still present in her relationship with God. Roots of doubt and unbelief have been exposed. And now He is going deeper to break her out of it.

Make no mistake about it—this has been the journey of the global Shulammite, the worldwide Body of Christ. From the very beginning, the early church dined at the Table of the Lord and was ushered into incredible joy and peace in the House of Wine. But very quickly, the roots of law and unbelief crept back in and the apostles spent much of their time coming against these things. As a matter of fact, several of the apostles themselves fell back into the law during the days of the early church! Since then, much of the church's journey has been about coming out from behind this wall.

The tragedy is that the old covenant law is no longer in effect. The rain is truly over and the winter is totally gone. But our unbelief veils us from experiencing this and so this veil must be dealt with.

And this is what the Song will address next.

10 The Fig Tree & Israel

The fig tree has ripened its figs...
(2:13a)

There is one more important truth hidden in Jesus's plea for the church to awaken to the realization that the era of the "wall" is over. In showing her several signs that a new day has come (such as the physical resurrection of the Christ or the Holy Spirit's presence among men), He adds one more symbolic point that we did not cover in the last chapter. He said that the "fig tree has ripened its figs." We will momentarily pause from the Shulammite's journey to look a little bit more in-depth at this one particular symbol.

All of the other symbols spoke to aspects of things that surrounded and followed Christ's death. This symbol of the fig tree is no different. If you were to study the fig tree throughout the Scriptures, you will find that it is most often a symbol for the nation of Israel. This reference to the fig tree in the Song of Songs also speaks about the state of Israel and relates directly to the prophecies Jesus Himself gave to Jerusalem and the overall nation.

The fig tree's "ripening" speaks of the nation's time for judgment, as He declared before His crucifixion. (Of course ripe fruit also speaks of harvest, but we are going to focus on the judgment end of it, which will make more sense as we progress.) In the book of Amos, the prophet is given a vision of a basket filled with summer fruit, and the Lord shows him that this symbol means that the nation of Israel was ripe for judgment and destruction (see Amos 8:2). The fig tree is a tree that bears its ripe fruit in the summer and its symbolism is the same in Solomon's Song.

When Jesus walked the earth, He spoke of the impending ripening of this "summer" judgment on Israel, which would come to pass in 70 A.D. when the Roman armies invaded and obliterated Jerusalem. A story is also told of Jesus's earthly ministry where He goes to a fig tree looking for fruit. When He does not find fruit, He curses the tree and it withers the next day. This is far more than a story highlighting the power of life and death in the tongue. This is also a symbolic picture of what Jesus had been warning Jerusalem about all along. If they did not turn towards grace and towards the final sacrifice of the Christ (and thus bear good fruit on the tree of the nation), they would render themselves cursed under the full penalty of the law.

Now let's be clear about the fact that Jesus has completely taken away the curse of the law on the cross. But for those who absolutely refuse the grace given to them (and thus demanding the law in its place), they could still reap the destruction that the law promises. Jesus made it abundantly clear that it was not His desire to bring accusation and judgment upon the people who were resisting His grace. He told the unbelieving Israelites that He would *not* accuse them before the Father, but rather Moses would—in whom they had "set their hope" (see Jn. 5:45). Moses represents the law that would accuse and bring destruction upon those who want to set their hope upon it and continue to live by eating from the Tree of Right and Wrong.

Deuteronomy 28 most clearly explains the curses that come upon a people who are not obeying the law, and these things came in full power in 70 A.D. as a result. The issue is made most clear in one of the parables Jesus told in Luke 13. There the Lord describes the story of a fig tree that was not bearing fruit and when summer came it continued to be found wanting. Time was given for it to bear fruit, but the tree was finally cut down when it was found wanting. The Romans would end up being the ones to bring the axe to the tree of Israel when they refused to turn to the Tree of Life and bear the fruit of true faith and repentance.

This is quite a weighty subject and I hesitated even bringing it up as it may raise questions that could distract us from the real intent of this book. I do not want this to dilute the message of intimacy and union. Nonetheless, Jesus does point to the ripening of Israel for harvest and judgment as one more sign of this new era. Consequently, there is an importance to looking deeper at this part of the text. Allow me then to say just a few more words about this "summer fruit" and hopefully connect it back to the Bride's journey...

The End of the Old Covenant Era

Jesus was crucified around 30 A.D. Right before His death on the cross as the sacrificial Lamb, Jesus spoke of the nation's coming destruction. He said this after weeping hysterically over the city, heartbroken that it would one day come to this. Jerusalem would reject the things that "make for peace" (Luke 19:42) and continue in the law instead of trusting in Him. More specifically, they would continue in the temple system of dead works, sacrificing animals to find forgiveness instead of trusting in Christ's final sacrifice.

This would be an insult to the Spirit of grace, because they would be regarding as unclean the true blood by which they were sanctified. The people would render themselves cursed simply because they stayed under the law (Heb. 6:8 and 10:29 clearly explain the preceding statements). As a result, Jerusalem would not enter into the rest and peace that Jesus's work on the cross provided. Within 40 years, the fig tree of Israel would be cut down. This happened exactly in 70 A.D., which was 40 years later. Hence, in Matthew 24, Jesus aptly spoke the following words:

Now learn the parable from the fig tree: when its branch has already become tender and puts forth its leaves, you know that

*summer is near; so, you too, when you see all these things, recognize that He is near, right at the door. Truly I say to you, **this generation** will not pass away until all these things take place. Heaven and earth will pass away, but My words will not pass away.*
(Matt. 24:32-35)

It is astounding to find that the same thing happened with the Israelites under Moses's leadership. They rejected the "promise" and within 40 years all of them died in the wilderness (see Numbers 14:34-35). So too, the people in Christ's day rejected the Promised Messiah and within the same period of time that generation was wiped out. The parallel between these two generations is uncanny.

The writer to the Hebrews prophesied about this and warned that the old covenant was "obsolete and...ready to disappear" (Heb. 8:20), and that the Lord would "judge His people" (Heb. 10:30) The writer penned those words around 64AD, giving a final plea for Hebrew believers to cling to the message of grace before the destruction of Jerusalem came upon them and the temple system was forever destroyed. Indeed, temple-based Judaism was never to be seen on the earth again. Though the stump of Israel would again rise as a nation 2000 years later, the full old covenant system was forever demolished. The "dead works" of animal sacrifices would now be likened to crucifying again the Son of God and putting Him to open shame (Heb. 6:6). The crop that grows out of the ground of such religion and unbelief is ripe for a curse of destruction (Heb. 6:8).

The Hebrew believers, like the Galatians, were being called out of the subtle hypnosis and *sleepiness* of law. And again, the global church all throughout history has fallen under this same spell as well. That is perhaps why many of the canonized epistles were so focused on calling the early church to stay away from the allure of going back to the law. The wall of the law brings nothing but death, while the Good News brings true life and rest.

You see, Israel's temple system and the old covenant itself were ripe to be shaken and destroyed so that the true temple of God could emerge. That true "temple" is the Shulammite, the church. It is the "one new man" consisting of both Jew and Gentile. The dividing wall of the old covenant and the dividing veil of the Holy of Holies had been torn to the ground, both spiritually and literally. He is fixing the Bride's gaze on a serious and sobering reality, something that symbolically manifested in 70 A.D. Like the writer of Hebrews, He is helping her to see the desperate need to get away from law and fear and to find shelter in the realm of grace and peace. He knows that if she stays behind her wall, it will lead to nothing but destruction.

So with all that being said, let us clearly see that now is indeed the time to leave the dividing wall, the veil of the Holy of Holies, and the old covenant itself. Now is the time to see that the Lord is risen and that the Holy Spirit is here. He is calling all people, which still includes the dear and beloved nation of Israel, to "come away" from the dividing wall of the Law, seeing that the fig tree was ripened and the temple system forever obliterated.

Now is the time to believe. And rest.

11 Foxes and Fear

O my dove, in the clefts of the rock,
In the secret place of the steep pathway,
Let me see your form,
Let me hear your voice;
For your voice is sweet,
And your form is lovely.
(2:14)

Treading deeper into the sounds and lyrics proceeding from this Song, we find yet again words of great beauty and encouragement flowing from the heart of the Shepherd. Now remember that He is in the process of calling her out from behind the wall, from behind the window of potential vision into a place of substance, reality, and fulfillment. It is as though He is preaching to her, trying to convince her of something of infinite importance. However, it has been made clear that the "burning of the sun" in other's vineyards has done much more damage than we may have originally suspected. The thinking behind her comments about her dark and Kedar-like skin goes much deeper. It is rooted in the very Tree of Good and Evil and the law system itself. Though she has tasted and seen that the Lord is good and His work is finished, that taste has not yet translated into a full and continuous meal.

Jesus continues His speech, moving from the signs of a new season to now speaking further about who she is and *where she is.* By saying that she is hidden in the "clefts of the rock" and in the "secret place of the steep pathway," He is showing her that the wall does not define her nor does it truly restrict her. We will look at both of these metaphors of the rock and the steep pathway to better understand our true location and position according to the Voice of truth.

You don't have to listen to many Christian hymns before you're reminded that Christ is the Rock on which you stand and the cleft of the rock in which you're hidden. These lyrics draw from the revelation Paul brought forth when he said that we are hidden in Christ, who is our Rock. The cleft of a rock represents a place of complete safety and protection.

The Shulammite was shown as still being in fear of the winter of sin and the rain of judgment. But in the clefts of His wounds on the cross, the hiding place of His merciful blood, we find that these things can no longer touch us. And so the Shepherd speaks with passion and clarity to the Bride who is standing behind the wall of enmity and disunion. He comes to her, reminding her that His blood and sacrifice have completely shielded her from wrath and from a darkened identity. She is found in the perfect peace and pleasure of the Father.

This leads to the revelation that she is also hidden in the steep pathway, which could also be translated as a staircase. This steep pathway might bring to mind the ladder that Jacob saw in Genesis 28, on which angels ascended and descended. It was a connection point between heaven and earth, an open heaven where Jacob received promises and revelation. Thousands of years later, we learned that Jesus is actually Jacob's true ladder (see Jn. 1:51). He is the one who completely unites heaven and earth. In Him all the portals of heaven are wide open and the resources of eternity can be released onto the earth. He demonstrated this Himself through a life of complete love (which is the very atmosphere of heaven) and of complete authority over sickness, sin, destructive weather, and demonic power. Jesus is the One who brings heaven to earth.

It is absolutely amazing to see that the Shulammite—who is hiding behind the law and is not abiding in the place of intimacy and truth—is declared to be located in this steep pathway as well! This might be hard to swallow, but there is an open heaven over your life, whether you believe it or not, or feel you have earned it or not. You do not have to break open the heavens, for Jesus already broke it open. In fact, *He is our open heaven*, and according to this Song, we are hidden in that place with Him. It is called a steep pathway because it reaches right up to the throne of God, where we are seated with Christ in victory and authority. Even the immature, doubting Christian stands in this position as well. It is only the wall of the law that keeps their eyes from seeing and experiencing it. The book of Proverbs tells us that the heart is the wellspring of all life. So if the heart is veiled by the wall of the old covenant and by fear, then the springs of eternal life will not freely flow.

What's happening here is that Jesus is expounding the written Word to the doubting Shulammite, unfolding the mysteries of the Scriptures in hopes that her eyes would be illuminated to what the Word has always pointed to. The imagery of rock clefts, pathways, and vineyards are laid throughout the Scriptures like puzzle pieces that are meant to come together and form one picture. The glorious picture is of Christ and Him crucified. He is now showing her this imagery so that she might come to see that she can really trust this too-good-to-be-true Gospel message in all of its fullness. She can trust it, because the Scriptures testify to it left and right.

> *But now apart from the Law, the righteousness of God has been manifested, **being witnessed by the Law and the Prophets**.*
> *(Rom. 3:21)*

This is what Jesus literally did after His resurrection when He appeared to His disciples. It says that He opened the Scriptures to them so that they would understand the biblical centrality of the Messiah's suffering and rising (see Luke 24:25-27, 44-45). Indeed, all of the Bible points to the work of the Lamb, and many times the Lord will use the Scriptures to awaken His doubting followers to the realities of our co-crucifixion and co-resurrection with Him. It is the scarlet thread woven throughout the Bible; the blood splattered throughout the "book of the Law" (see Heb. 9:19).

Out from Hiding

After expounding on these things, the Lord asks to hear her voice and see her form. He speaks this by acknowledging how incredibly beautiful and lovely she is. It's been said a million times through multitudes of sermons and messages, but we need to hear it again and again... If we could understand how beautiful and lovely we are to the Lord, it would change everything! This is the song of eternity that the Lord carries as He knocks on the doors of our hearts and calls us to listen closely and repeatedly.

The Shulammite—the church—is the one who is hidden in His sacrifice and who abides in heavenly realms even while walking on the earth. She is washed and purified. There is now a power in her voice and a strength in her form that she has not yet realized. All of this beauty and loveliness is not some pick-me-up encouragement or flattery from the Lord. It is a genuine word that is truer than the ground upon which we stand. In light of this, He tells her to "come out." There is no religion here, no expectation of performance, or the giving of a legalistic command. It is only the call for her to know her beauty and to be who she already is. *Come out of hiding and shame and be yourself!* This Song is poetically articulating the spirit and heart of the Gospel and the true Christian life.

There is no gaining a beautiful form or acquiring a lovely voice for the Lord. He declares that her form is already lovely to Him and her voice is already sweet. So many of us pray to the Lord and beg Him to make us more holy—more "lovely and sweet" in our speech (voice) and in our actions (form). This is often a heartfelt and honorable prayer, but it usually arises from the "lack of knowledge" that was found earlier in the Song. The Lord wants her to know so desperately that she is already holy. He calls her to simply step out and *trust* this. This is the righteousness of faith.

Earlier in the Song, the Bride was simply dipping her feet into the endless oceans of grace. Her eyes were being turned away from the murky ponds of religion and a false identity and she was given a great view of the sea of God's love (and her reflection within it). But now a reckoning has come and the call is to truly believe these things and thus to naturally live in light of them—moving from toe to ankle to waist in the bliss of total acceptance and union.

Very often, a person gets a revelation of grace or of Christ's finished work and they get really happy and freed up from a lot of religious expectations. But when the rubber hits the road and "life happens," the subtly of old ways and old thinking creeps back in. We have seen this happen in the Shulammite's journey and many of us can testify to it as well. We might fall short in a certain area or we see something in the natural that does not line up with the beauty and holiness of Jesus, and so we go back into hiding. We turn back to the safety of old and dirty ponds that we believe to be more fitting for our performance and experience. The message of grace, while still pounding in our ears like waves against the shore, seems a million miles away.

Sometimes this turning back into hiding involves an inward penance (an old term for paying for one's sins). We punish ourselves in an effort to inwardly atone for missing whatever standards we've set for ourselves. Though most people in this post-reformation era wouldn't be quick to admit this, it still occurs within many hearts. We allow ourselves to feel distant and when we do certain things (correct our actions, pray more, fast more, etc.), then we can feel "close to the Lord" again. We feel accepted because of our behavior more than the blood of Jesus (even though we may verbally proclaim that the blood is the only ground of our acceptance before God). Once again, let me say that I am not speaking against correcting our actions or prayer and spiritual disciplines. I am simply talking about the religious motivation that sometimes attaches itself to these behaviors. We turn these things into a system instead of living in the freedom of the Gospel and of simply being ourselves in Christ.

But the Shepherd speaks to His slumbering church. He sings out His call for freedom:

No more! No more back and forth in the confidence of My love. No more hiding and shame gripping your heart. No more fear of unrelenting darkness hiding in the corners of your soul. And no more thinking that you need to do something to be near to Me.

I am a constant Drink. The Drink is not located on a far off mountaintop so that only the religious elite or astutely disciplined can attain it. The Drink lies in the closest place you could possibly imagine—your very inner being and heart! You are lovely, you are beautiful, and you are sanctified and holy. These are not theological terms to argue and debate over. They are the fruit of my intense suffering when you were hidden in the cleft of My wounds. These words are spirit and they are life. So rise up, My love.

The very fact that we are hidden in the pathway and in the cleft of the rock reveals that we are truly one with Christ. We are His image and likeness, even when we feel that a wall of fear surrounds us. And when we embrace this constant oneness with the Lord, striving and fear effortlessly dissipate.

Foxes in the Vineyard

*Catch the foxes for us
The little foxes that are ruining the vineyards,
While our vineyards are in blossom.*

*My beloved is mine, and I am his;
He pastures his flock among the lilies.
Until the cool of the day and the shadows flee away,
Turn, my beloved, and be like a gazelle,
Or a young stag on the mountains of Bether.*
(2:15-17)

We arrive next at the Bride's response to the Lord's long tune as He continues to beckon her into freedom. She gives the reason for why she is not out there enjoying the blossoming vineyards of the Spirit and of resurrection life. And make no mistake about it, those "vineyards *are in blossom.*" In other words, the life and fruit of the Spirit is present and busting forth. The "fruit of the Spirit" is the very divine nature, and the Scriptures say that we are able *now* to partake of this divine nature. We are called to eat the fruit of the Promised Land, which is love, joy, peace, patience, and all the other beautiful facets found in the face and heart of our Father. We are reflections and image-bearers, not in theory, but in the crisp light of day right here on planet earth.

Unbelief would love to keep these things at a distance. We think that perhaps after years of laboring in the fields that this fruit will manifest, or maybe after some prophecy of a far-off revival is fulfilled. But no, the vineyards of the Holy Spirit are already blossoming because of the work of Christ. Revival is here and now. But something is obviously holding the Bride back from fully "partaking" of this reviving fruit. She describes this something as *foxes*...

In Solomon's day, foxes were a serious problem for grape vineyards. Small foxes would creep through the fences and barriers surrounding the vineyards and eat away at the new fruit coming forth from the branches. So the Shulammite is looking at her life and saying that the fruit is being eaten away. Foxes of some sort are ruining it from appearing. She hears the Lord speak of her beauty and holiness. She knows that she is a branch and He is the vine. But now she sees some major contradictions in her outward life. We might paraphrase her words as follows:

Lord, you may say that I am beautiful and lovely and hidden in the rock, but when I look at my life I do not see the fruit that equates to Your words. Please Lord, get rid of the things that hinder me from living in the purity and holiness you declare over me.

I should probably go ahead and give a long admonition of the different things these foxes could represent, such as lust, greed, or envy. But I am actually going to hold back on that for now. The reason for this is that I want to get at the real root issue of what allows these foxes entrance in the first place. I also want to keep the focus on the overarching flow of dialogue between the Shulammite and the Lord. Remember that the Lord is calling forth her identity and reminding her of His loving atonement. She is then responding negatively once again after seeing the lack of outward fruit in her life.

Now dealing with different foxes is a very important part of our journey. But it is a minor issue in comparison to the grander theme emerging in the music of this Song. That theme involves trust and faith in the Gospel and confidence in God's love. The biggest fight is not against sin in and of itself, but against unbelief in the Gospel and in who we truly are. Really, the most ugly fox in our vineyard is the fox that denies the finished work of Christ and disbelieves His words of love and truth. This will be more clearly defined as we finish up the chapter.

Turn Away...

Thankfully, the Shulammite will acknowledge one of the central truths she has learned up to this point. She declares, "My Beloved is mine and I am His." Even in the midst of her doubts, she is at a point where she recognizes that He is her good Shepherd and that she truly belongs to Him. The theme of love continues to strum like consistent chords in the Song and she has learned much since her first cry for the kiss of the Spirit upon her life. But as far as knowing how close the Lord truly is to her and how deep His Gospel goes... that is another story.

The sleep of religion and illusion is what continues in her responses to the Lord. She may intellectually know the truth, but to truly walk it out seems like a distant promise. The fear and the lies also seem too strong to break. And so she responds by telling Him to turn away from her. She does want to walk with Him in the life of manifested victory upon the hills and the mountains.

"Turn, my beloved," she tragically speaks. She is choosing to stay behind her wall.

Looking at everything we have seen thus far, we find that she says all of this simply because she does not believe that she is able to walk with the Lord in the capacity that He is calling her to. She absolutely loves the Lord and has prayed for that life of adventure, intimacy, and freedom. But she fears her ability to follow through and perhaps still wonders if some raincloud of judgment might come upon her life. She also fears the foxes, which go hand in hand with the symbol of winter and its icy lock over the fruit of the Spirit in her life.

The root of why she can't believe that she can step into this new springtime of freedom is hidden in the final line of this part of the Song. This is perhaps one of the most important things to notice in this portion of the text. It is something that has been building all along. Hidden behind those chords of love have been darker musical notes that communicate something of the Shulammite's inner belief system. We have seen hints of this belief system coming out throughout the Song, but now its dark notes will come out in full blast.

First, she says that she is waiting for the "day" to fully come. She speaks of a day when the shadows of deception and fear will flee away. At that point she says that perhaps she will be ready to walk with Jesus in the fullness of His life and grace. But until that day comes, she tells her Beloved to turn away. This ties back to the belief system that wants to wait to die in order to experience the righteousness and rest of the Gospel. It relegates the life of God to the day of the final resurrection of the dead. Or it could simply refer to the lie that victory elusively waits far out in some prophetic future instead of here and now. Doubt and deception are leading to all kinds of excuses as to why she can't come away with Jesus on the mountains and hills. And the reason for all of this doubt emerges at the end of this particular verse...

The Shulammite describes her Beloved as being on the mountains of Bether.

Bether, in the Hebrew, can be translated as *separation*...

I know I am on the verge of belaboring this point. We have already said it over and over again and my hope is that it is not just becoming a concept in the mind that we read easily and then bypass. However, since it is brought up again, we need to say it loud and clear once more. The Shulammite, or the young church, still sees separation between her and Jesus. She still sees Him as "other." Her mind has not truly been renewed to the truth that she is *one spirit* with Him. Much has already been said on this, but all of it goes back to that dividing wall. She has something incredibly significant and eternally impactful to learn. She must see that it is "no longer I who live, but Christ lives in me" (Gal. 2:20).

The Shulammite will go through much frustration and pain because of this issue of a perceived mountain of separation. This is the larger issue that trumps any one particular fox. Foxes are only allowed entrance because of this deception in the first place. The holes in our fences (where we fail to guard our hearts, the wellspring of life) communicate one main thing... *Ignorance.* Ignorance of who we are and of who God is...

*So this I say, and affirm together with the Lord, that you walk no longer just as the Gentiles also walk, in the futility of **their mind**, being darkened in **their understanding,** excluded from the life of God **because of the ignorance that is in them,** because of the hardness of **their heart**...*
(Eph. 4:17-18)

12 The Religious System

On my bed night after night I sought him
Whom my soul loves;
I sought him but did not find him.
I must arise now and go about the city;
In the streets and in the squares
I must seek him whom my soul loves.
I sought him but did not find him.
(3:1-2)

L iving under the "sleep" of separation and fear, the Shulammite begins to search for her Beloved. She is longing to taste the sweet wine and the delicious apples that she encountered in her earlier experiences in the story. She is looking for her Bridegroom and is still seeking after a permanent union. Yet she speaks something very telling at the onset of this search. She says that she is *on her bed* while this searching takes place. In other words, she is looking for Him while still asleep.

Even though it appears the Bride is setting about to do a noble task in seeking the Lord Jesus, we will find that the dividing wall is still present within her search. The wall, the bed, the searching... all of it points to the same dilemma. It is the unrenewed mindset of estrangement from God and perhaps some remaining sense of hostility between her and the Father. So many of us are also "seeking God" in this way—asleep to the full wonders of what happened at Calvary where everything that hinders intimacy and oneness was removed. Intimacy is always out of reach when there is even the slightest sense of inferiority, or potential resentment and distance from the other party. So in this place she searches diligently, *but does not find Him.* Twice she will say this.

The Shulammite eventually goes into "the city" to search for her Beloved. Over the years, multitudes of commentators on the Song of Songs have attributed the city to the corporate church. So in order to find the One her soul loves and longs for, the One she is designed to know on an intimate level, she will begin to go to the church. And there she does not find him either...

Now I want to be very clear as to how I communicate the following. Being connected with a body of believers is absolutely vital and the Lord does amazing things in the church, whether it's in connection to an organized institution (yes, God's still doing great things there) or the organic movements of people gathering and fellowshipping around Christ outside of the establishment. Regardless of where it happens, we are called to connect with people and it is there we will find the Lord in one another.

But the Shulammite's fruitless searching though the "city" of the church speaks of something much deeper than just connecting with other believers. It ultimately reveals that she is looking to the "church system" itself to provide the life and intimacy she craves. She goes into the different sections of the city—its "streets" and "squares"—and is thus searching every corner of it to find him. She is going to every single thing the church has to offer in order to encounter the living and abiding presence of God. But again, this is initially fruitless.

This could be compared to the believer today who goes from ministry to ministry, conference to conference, church to church, and bible study to bible study looking for the One their soul craves. At times they do indeed find Him as is revealed later on in the Song, but many times it is a tiring and emotionally up-and-down endeavor. Even though she finds Him later on, we will see that this is a temporary discovery that does not lead to truly "coming away" into resurrection life and power. Nor does it lead to a consistent communion with the Lord.

There are whole seas of people who are searching for God in religious systems, including those that carry the banner of Christ's name. They search and search, night after night, but do not truly find Him there. They may learn about Him and gain ideas about Him. They may even brush into His presence here and there. But the Eden life eludes them and they know in their hearts that there must be something more.

Broad is the Path

Once again, we can find parallels to the Shulammite's journey when looking at the movement of the church throughout history. There was a period of falling away from the message of grace during the latter days of the early church. Following this was the beginning of systematized Christianity. The sleeping Bride went to the "city" to find her Beloved. A city of religious structures was built and it became the place that a majority of people went to in order to find God. The Hebraic temple system and the Levitical priesthood were reconstructed in new and upgraded ways, and people were given new religious rituals to follow. They may have no longer sacrificed bulls and goats, but they still went to their new Levite priests to find forgiveness and connection with God, instead of confidently heading into the Holy of Holies to enjoy God's presence for themselves. This happened in Rome and in many other sectors of the world where Christianity spread. But the true Bride has never been satisfied with such a life.

It is interesting to read this passage from the King James Version, which says that the Bride went into the streets and "into the broad ways" to search for the King. This is a more literal translation of the Hebrew word for "squares." It is a reminder of Jesus's words, who said that the way to life is narrow while the majority of the world traverses the *broad* paths that lead to destruction (see Mat. 7:13-14). We have traditionally interpreted this statement as defining the narrow path to heaven, but Jesus is simply speaking of the path to *zoe* life. He used this same Greek word for life in John 17:3, where He said that eternal life is to "know God." There are indeed many people who are heading for heaven and yet they do not intimately know the Father and His Christ here on earth. Jesus is creating a dichotomy between the broad paths of religion, which lead to nothing but fruitlessness and destruction, and the narrow path of intimacy with God and eternal life within. Here, the Bride is fruitlessly searching for God through the broad ways of religion.

To be clear, this is not a hidden attack against the Roman Catholic Church, structured Protestant Christianity, or the Eastern Orthodox Church (though the broad paths of destruction can be found in all three camps). The "broad ways" are simply our re-building of the tower of Babel, which gives people a system to clean themselves up or reach the heavens and find God, instead of giving them the pure Gospel of grace that declares the finished work of Jesus on their behalf. So this is not an attack against the church. There are plenty of books available where you can study the history or debate about it further. Right now, we are solely looking at the Shulammite's journey to freedom and the narrow path of grace that will lead her into her full inheritance in Christ.

The watchmen who make the rounds in the city found me,
And I said, 'Have you seen him whom my soul loves?'
Scarcely had I left them when I found him whom my soul loves.
I held onto him and would not let him go
Until I had brought him to my mother's house,
And into the room of her who conceived me.
(3:3-4)

Eventually it says that she comes to the "watchmen" of the city and inquires of them as to where she may find her Beloved. Here we find that she is going to leadership (the watchmen) in hopes of finding that deeper connection and intimacy with Jesus. But it is quite interesting that when she leaves the "watchmen" she immediately finds the One she was looking for. So as she disconnects from the leaders of the religious system, she begins to find the true presence of Christ.

Now this is not a hidden attack against leadership either. This only reveals that true and godly Shepherds will always point away from themselves, teaching the sheep how to feed from the Good Shepherd Himself. Good leaders do not subtly teach us to rely on them, but on our union with the Lord and the indwelling Holy Spirit. False watchmen (and this is sometimes unintentional) may get God's people locked into their own teachings and leadership (or into an overall church system) instead of the abiding and intimate presence of the Lord.

The Song of Songs is singing a higher tune than the average Christian has experienced over the centuries. That is not meant to sound elitist or as giving some "special knowledge," so please do not hear that. Let's at least agree that the life Jesus demonstrated and the life that the apostles tapped into has not been experienced by a majority of people in Christendom. So this is only meant to call out the fact that perhaps our systems and doctrines within the "city" do not provide what we truly need.

We are speaking here of a life that is rooted in our union with Christ that does not lean upon a church system and church leaders to find its substance. It freely fellowships with the Body, serves the saints, and submits to others in love. But the church *system*, including its leaders, are not our Bread and Wine. Whether inside or outside church buildings and structures, the Shulammite is finding the need to move beyond the systems of man. This is a path laid out for the courageous and for those willing to let go of the status quo.

With that being said, it is important to note that the watchmen of the cities in Solomon's day would usually stand by the outer gates and walls. This is all painting a very specific picture for us. When she leaves the watchmen, she has already looked everywhere else, including every street and square of the city. This means that she has nowhere else to go but beyond the city gates and walls. And the text says that it is very quickly after this that she finds the One her soul loves.

The Shulammite, after searching through every corner of the city, finally goes to the outskirts of the religious system in order to find the One she adores. Has it not been the case throughout church history that those who were on the fringes of the religious establishment were the ones who often paved the way into new territory and into greater restoration of the Kingdom? This is what the Shulammite is doing as well. Very often, those who are absolutely desperate for true intimacy and relationship with God go way outside the bounds and systems where everyone else comfortably sets up camp. We love to honor the men and women who did this, but none of us realize how controversial and difficult it would have been to stand with them in the days of their pioneering work.

All of this is not a call to just get up and abandon our churches. The Lord is faithful to speak to our hearts as to where to be connected. Rather, this is a call to realize that the Lord lies outside the broad ways that man sets up. This is not even just about our church structures and programs, but it is about the things that are often taught and believed within those structures. Nothing that is taught in the streets and squares brought her into the full and true presence of her Bridegroom. Outside of man's systems there is a revelation of union with Christ, of the reality of His shed blood, and the pure grace that brought us into the Holy of Holies. Look at the following Scripture with fresh eyes:

Do not be carried away by varied and strange teachings; for it is good for the heart to be strengthened by grace, not by foods (the religious prescriptions of man), *through which those who were so occupied were not benefited. We have an altar from which those who serve the tabernacle have no right to eat. For the bodies of those animals whose blood is brought into the holy place by the high priest as an offering for sin, are burned outside the camp.*

*Therefore Jesus also, that He might sanctify the people through His own blood, suffered outside the gate. So, let us go out to Him **outside the camp**, bearing His reproach. For here we do not have a lasting city, but we are seeking the city which is to come.*
(Heb. 13:9-14, parenthesis mine)

In going beyond the city and "outside the camp," the Bride will suffer the reproach of being different than everyone else who is still locked in the system. But she will also come again into an enjoyment of the Lord's sweet and refreshing presence. And when she does, there is nothing more she wants but to stay there.

When one freshly encounters the Lord there is nothing like it. She absolutely loves His presence and also wants to bring Him into her "mother's house." When you begin to truly taste of the Lord's manifest presence (which is Life itself), you want nothing more than Mother Church (and her task-master sons) to experience that same thing as well. As a reminder from the first chapter, the mother represents Israel and the overall church. That is what we are seeing played out here. The Shulammite has personally encountered the Lord and now she wants to share her experience with others amongst God's people who may still be trapped in a system of religion.

And Yet Still Asleep

I adjure you, O daughters of Jerusalem
By the gazelles or by the hinds of the field,
That you will not awaken my love
Until she pleases
(3:5)

Unfortunately, there is still a spiritual slumbering that continues. Even though she is having these encounters with the Lord and she again comes into His presence, the Shulammite is still not awake to the fullness of who she is and the truth that God is bringing to her. This brings up an important point, with which we'll close this particular chapter...

Do you know that people can see miracles and have encounters with God's presence and yet still miss the awakened life of rest and the enjoyment of union with God? It is akin to the Israelites out in the wilderness, circling and circling but never fully arriving in the Promised Land. You can imagine them at times circling very close to the Promised Land to the point of smelling its scents and beholding its views. But there was also always a journeying away, going deeper into the wilderness until a fresh view of the Promised Land could return for another short season.

Such is the life of religion. It is going through cycles of feeling close to God one day and then feeling a million miles away the next and thus needing to re-up our prayers and efforts (and our searching through the "streets and squares" of the church) in order to find Him again. It is a religious system of sacrificing the bulls of our own efforts and washing ourselves at the brazen altar day in and day out, instead of abiding in the Holy of Holies, forever cleansed from a guilty conscience.

I believe this speaks to multitudes of us who are searching for the One our soul loves in the highways and byways of spirituality and church life. Those of us who are looking for the divine kiss of life and the place of rest and righteousness (even those of us who are on the fringes and outskirts of the religious establishment). Please do not receive any condemnation from this. Remember that this is the journey of the Shulammite, who represents the whole church. There is value to be found in all our spiritual excursions, even the ones in the wilderness. The Lord is with us on this journey and He has even prophesied the church's wilderness wandering through this Song. This was written during the days of Solomon, a few thousand years before the church was actually birthed. The Lord knew the journey His people would take and was committed to seeing them through it

Remember also that the era of Solomon was the era of the Temple's construction. Solomon built the Temple and he wrote this Song around the same time period. Through the son of David, God was declaring a journey of construction and love that would take place far out in the future. So do not beat yourself up if your own journey is not where you think it should be. The Lord will finish His Temple and He will have an awakened and radiant Bride (or, in better terms, He will reveal and manifest the beauty of His Temple and Bride).

Don't lose heart or grow impatient, for a day to the Lord is as a thousand years and a thousand years as a day (2 Pet. 3:8 & Ps. 90:4). We are in the "third day" since Christ's resurrection and extraordinary things typically happen on the third day. The call to awake will increase in volume and deepen in its pull. Like the call of the Spirit to the deceased body of Christ after two days in the grave, so the Spirit calls to the corporate Body of Christ stuck in the grave of fear and illusion for two days in God's timing. After 2000 years, the Body of Christ is being called to awake and step into the fullness of the resurrection life that Jesus purchased for us to walk in. This is the call of the Spirit and the Song of our Beloved.

From Religion to Rest

Perhaps condemnation is not what some readers are feeling. Perhaps some are instead feeling a sense of frustration with this portion of the book. Perhaps the need to defend the life of religious effort and "city-searching" is coming forth. One might rightly argue that many who live such a life of pursuing God's presence in these ways (as opposed to the one who is resting in His abiding presence and is no longer "seeking" in a striving sense) experience great miracles and breakthroughs in their lives... I will not argue that. But let me remind you that while the Israelites were wandering in the wilderness God did many miracles—most of which were more spectacular than what we've seen in some of the most powerful ministries today (and that was under the old covenant). God's mercy, provision, and protection still exist in the wilderness. But the wilderness is not our ultimate destination.

There are many people living a wilderness Christianity (either in the city or on the fringes) who do not believe in the full implications of Christ's finished work and our complete union with God. Yet they still experience miracles, heavenly encounters, and provision. This is the Lord's mercy. But there is indeed a Promised Land where we rest from our religious labors. We eat of vineyards that we did not plant or toil over and receive "land and homes" that we did not labor to build (see Josh. 24:13). In other words, there is a place where we receive His life effortlessly and plentifully—by grace and not by a system. It is a place called "it is finished." This is a Sabbath rest for the people of God that flows from a constant source of Bread and Wine.

In this chapter of the Song, the Bride is shown to still be working to somehow maintain God's presence in her life. To some extent, she believes that she is the one who is in control of this union. Once she found His presence, the text says that she would not "let Him go"—as though she were the one with the hold on Him and not the other way around. This partly reveals that she believes this union is dependent upon herself. She is holding onto Him and choosing not to let Him go and it is from that mindset that she believes she will fully carry the Lord's presence to her mother, the church. Unfortunately, this is not what will initially happen.

The Bride is intensely seeking after her Beloved, but it is still from a framework of self-effort—the place of sleep. This is something that countless people can relate to. Now for many this is truly done out of love and I believe the Lord honors this and loves the passion in His seeking church. Again, there is not even a hint of condemnation in these words. (Did you hear any condemnation in the voice of the Bridegroom as He spoke to His beloved behind her wall?)

Nonetheless, this is only one phase of the Bride's journey. It is not the destination and it is not our true portion and inheritance.

There is a place of real rest where we truly "find" what we're looking for and never thirst or hunger again (as Jesus promised). A place where we release control and trust that He is the One who eternally holds us, and not the other way around. This does not lead to apathy as some would accuse this message of doing. We will see later on in the text that this actually leads to the greatest amount of fruitfulness one could possibly imagine. But that's getting ahead of ourselves...

For now, let's heed the Lord's gentle singing over His Bride. There is an awakening coming that He anticipates. It's an awakening that we can all anticipate and look forward to, where we all come into the full stature of Christ and the true awareness of what really happened at Calvary. He speaks to the Daughters of Jerusalem, who represent all those who have come from Israel's womb, whether those who truly know the Lord or those who just attend church and are at the beginning of their spiritual journey. He tells them not to awaken His Bride until she is ready.

There is a mystery and depth in what He is saying here and so we need to go beyond the face value of these final words. Jesus is speaking to the church (the Daughters of Jerusalem) about the true church (the Shulammite). In other words, He is speaking to those still asleep about their own awakened destiny and calling. Awakening is indeed coming, but it must be out of love. It must come from the heart and from the pure springs of grace and faith. And that is the journey that He will continue to lead the Shulammite on. He is calling her to the outskirts of the religious system and the self-defeating doctrines of man. This is the beginning of her awakening, but it is not the end.

13 The Wedding Procession

What is this coming up from the wilderness
Like columns of smoke
Perfumed with myrrh and frankincense,
With all scented powders of the merchant
Behold, it is the traveling couch of Solomon;
Sixty mighty men around it,
Of the mighty men of Israel.
All of them wielders of the sword, experts in war;
Each man has his sword at his side,
Guarding against the terrors of the night.
(3:6-8)

The Shulammite has gone beyond the bounds of man's religion and has moved past a relationship with God mediated by leaders. She is on the outskirts of the city and has gratefully re-encountered the Lord's presence. Though there are still elements of self-effort at play, and still a journey of complete awakening set before her, the Shulammite is slowly "coming up from the wilderness." She is moving into the Eden life that she desired from the beginning.

A glorious vision will be given at this point in the Song that comes as a type of pause in the journey. For a moment in time, Solomon will paint us a picture of a royal palanquin emerging from the wilderness. A palanquin was a travelling carriage that typically held a king or queen. It contained a comfortable seat for the leader and was carried on the shoulders of men by means of poles. In this particular scene, we are beholding the King, the Lord Jesus Himself, "on the day of His wedding." This is a wedding procession that is moving forward in triumph and victory.

At the end of this scene, the daughters of Zion are invited to come and gaze at the sight before them. In their gazing, wisdom and revelation will be given. You, beloved reader, are a child of Zion as well. And so the Holy Spirit also extends this invitation to you. Come and gaze at this passage and get a clearer look of what is indeed "coming up from the wilderness." As we look deeply into this picture and allow ourselves to focus in on its imagery, a storehouse of wisdom and revelation will take root in our own souls.

Fragrant Smoke

As one begins to gaze out across the wilderness and beholds the emerging procession, the first thing their eyes would see would be great columns of smoke billowing forward. As they continued to look at this approaching smoke, its scent would soon wisp through their senses as it travelled across the wind. After taking in the fragrance, the onlooker would discern it to be myrrh and frankincense. The sight of the smoke and its proceeding aroma would surely bring a sense of wonder and curiosity as the wedding procession approached.

In looking at this passage spiritually, the columns (or pillars) of smoke speak to us first and foremost about the sweet presence of God who leads His church like He led Israel by cloud and fire. This was in a different wilderness where God had led the procession of the wandering Israelites by an immense pillar of cloud during the day. And even in the church's wilderness wandering of unbelief, the Lord has been intimately present with us as He leads us towards the fullness of His Christ-centered plans. As a result, this entire scene of the travelling palanquin gives us a visual of the words of Paul in the New Testament:

But thanks be to God, who always leads us in triumphal proces-
sion in Christ and through us spreads everywhere the fragrance
of the knowledge of Him.
(2 Cor. 2:14 NIV)

We are indeed *in Christ* and so this scene is just as much
an image of the victorious Christ as it is His church—for the
Shulammite, just as the church, is the one who has been joined
to Him on His "wedding day." We are called to be a people led by
the presence of God as we enjoy our union with Him. We are not
to be led by programs or by man's logic and reason. The presence
of God alone is our leader and source.

Like the trained nose can discern deeper and more hidden
scents, the onlooker of this scene might detect something deeper
about this imagery of the smoke, especially as they take note of the
myrrh and incense. It has been clearly laid out that myrrh speaks of
Christ's death. Frankincense represents intercession, which speaks
about Christ's life, for "He *always lives* to make intercession" for
us (Heb. 7:25). Therefore, this beautiful fragrance emerging from
the wilderness is that of both the death and life of our Lord. After
saying that God leads us in triumphal procession, Paul immediately said that we spread the fragrance of the knowledge *of Him*,
and that this fragrance is both life and death (see 2 Cor. 2:15). In
our victorious march forward with Christ we are surrounded by
the knowledge of His death and resurrection. The church's wedding procession, as she exits the wilderness, releases this fragrant
knowledge everywhere.

The Host of Heaven

As one continues to gaze on this scene, the next thing they
would see is a large number of people surrounding the travelling
carriage. As they look closer, they would see that these are sixty
mighty men with swords on their sides, offering protection from
"the terrors of the night." Now this could be interpreted in several

ways, but it seems the core theme here is that of complete security. We are in a *triumphant* wedding procession where we are completely surrounded and protected by the mighty host of the King.

This host is comprised of the very angels of heaven, for the Scriptures speak over and over again of how the Lord is surrounded by a great angelic presence and He oversees whole armies of them. These angels watch over us and protect us in our journey forward. Solomon is now giving us a visual of Psalm 91 in action, where his father David wrote about those who dwell in the secret place of God. The secret place is the dwelling of union and intimacy with the King. It speaks of one who abides in that travelling palanquin with Jesus. Those who dwell there "will not be afraid of the terror by night, or of the arrow that flies by day...for He will give His angels charge concerning you" (Ps. 91:5, 11).

The wilderness surrounding Jerusalem in Solomon's day could be a dangerous place filled with wild animals and thieves. If the Bride were to look out of her travelling caravan and focus on the wilderness and its terrors, she could easily lose heart and forget where she was seated. Such is the case with many of us. We are seated right in the presence of our Bridegroom and King, surrounded by the unconquerable host of heaven. Nothing can truly harm us. And yet in our deceptive daze, we can often focus on wild beasts outside and forget the pillar of smoke, the host of heaven, and our glad and joyful Bridegroom who leads us in triumph.

Seated with Christ

King Solomon has made for himself a sedan chair
From the timber of Lebanon
He made its posts of silver, its back of gold
And its seat of purple fabric
With its interior lovingly fitted out
By the daughters of Jerusalem.
(3:9-10)

Letting our vision then focus in a little tighter, we would see the centerpiece of this entire scene. Beyond the pillars of smoke and the mighty host surrounding the palanquin, we would start to get a clearer vision of the carriage itself and specifically its "sedan chair." This is the seat upon which the King sits and it draws our minds to another important "seat" within the Scriptures. In fact, this particular seat is the most important chair there ever was...

This is the Mercy Seat.

In Exodus 25, Moses began to lay out the plans for the tabernacle, which was a moving structure for worship and interaction with God while the people were out in the wilderness. He received the blueprints for this tabernacle from God Himself, and we know now that these blueprints were a heavenly pattern and symbol for something much greater (see Heb. 8:5). The blueprints contained three sections, which would later be used as the building plans for the temple. There was an outer court area where people could come and bring sacrifices to the priests. There was then the "Holy Place" where only the priests could go, which contained a lampstand, a table for bread, and an altar for fragrant incense. Then, through a veil, was the Most Holy Place containing the Ark of the Covenant. Two gold cherubim figures surrounded the Ark of the Covenant and on its top was the Mercy Seat where the High Priest would sprinkle sacrificial blood.

The Ark of the Covenant, and the Mercy Seat itself, was a focal point for the Hebrew people. It was known as the Lord's dwelling place as they moved through the wilderness. It was the most precious thing in the world to them. They knew it to be the very throne of God and the seat of His presence. When the Israelites moved the Ark of the Covenant through the wilderness, the priests would carry it on poles. It was God's palanquin!

The parallels between Moses's tabernacle and Solomon's wedding procession are remarkable. In the tabernacle, there was fragrant smoke and incense surrounding the Most Holy Place, just as fragrant smoke surrounds Solomon's carriage. If one were to gaze on Moses's tabernacle and look deeper, they would go beyond the veil and see the host of heaven—mighty cherubim—surrounding the Mercy Seat. Solomon's host surrounded his seat as well. The literal Ark of the Covenant was then built by Israelites, who brought sacrificial offerings of gold and silver to provide for its materials. The "daughters of Jerusalem lovingly fitted out" the interior of Solomon's carriage. The two parallel one another completely.

The Eternal Covenant

Go forth, O daughters of Zion
And gaze on the King Solomon with the crown
With which his mother has crowned him
On the day of his wedding
And on the day of his gladness of heart
(3:10)

So this is where we begin to understand what is really going on here. The Mercy Seat and the sedan chair point to the same reality. For thousands of years the Israelites had followed the Tabernacle system—yet in one stroke of the pen Solomon takes away the *veil* and gives us a poetic picture of what it was always about... A "wedding day."

Marriage involves a covenant. And it is on the Ark *of the Covenant* that God takes His seat. Besides speaking to us today, Solomon is also giving the Hebrew people a higher vision and understanding of the tabernacle that moved through the wilderness. It was never about an ongoing worship service with different duties, rituals, and sacrifices. Perhaps that's what was seen from an outside observer. But for those with eyes to see, those who choose to "gaze" even further, they would behold something much greater. The tabernacle and its innermost contents always pointed to the place that the Lord Himself would sit in covenantal marriage with His Bride. Even when Moses was receiving his blueprints on the mountain, it was always pointing to a love story of oneness and grace.

The church today needs to gaze into the Word like never before and move beyond the outward and artificial elements of the faith. Many are still stuck in the tabernacle of religious duties and services, and they are missing the higher meaning of it all. It was never meant to be about a religious system of drawing near to God. Ultimately, everything pointed to Jesus and our true union with Him. We need to focus our vision further, which may mean setting our gaze even beyond good things like the angels of heaven or some of the typical services and duties of the Christian life. At the center of it all there is a simple and intimate connection with Jesus. This is a connection sealed by the blood on the Mercy Seat.

The sedan chair upon which Solomon sat is described as being made of "purple fabric." In Hebrew, this is a word that could actually signify the colors of both red and purple. The color purple is often symbolically related to authority in the Bible. The red of course speaks to the sprinkling of Jesus's blood. How freeing and wondrous it is to realize that Jesus's authority is established upon the place of mercy! In other words, Jesus takes His seat of authority on the basis of our redeemed innocence. "When He made purification of sins, He sat down," the Scriptures say (Heb. 1:3). Our marriage to Him is true and valid because we have been made innocent and new in his eyes. His blood has forever sealed this covenant of marriage and love. The Passion Translation brings a sweet and illuminating description of what Solomon is communicating here:

> *The King made this mercy seat for Himself*
> *Out of the finest wood that will not decay.*
> *Pillars of smoke, like silver mist—*
> *A canopy of glory dwells above it.*
> *The place where they sit is sprinkled with crimson.*
> *Yes, love and mercy cover this carriage*
> *Blanketing this tabernacle-throne.*
> *The King Himself has made it for those who will become His bride!*
> *(Sgs. 3:9-10 TPT)*

To see the center of this palanquin is to see and behold David's "one thing," which is the greatest thing we could ever encounter (Ps. 27:4). It is the secret place of the Most High and the shadow of the Almighty. It is the place of the covenantal love of God.

But there is something else to be seen for those who continue to gaze...

A Glad and Happy God

There, in the midst of the smoke, the angels, and the mercy seat, is the King Himself. Now we may have seen His overall stature and finally gotten a glimpse of His glory as He sits confidently on the seat of mercy and authority. But if we were to look more deeply and behold His very face and the details therein, we would see something beyond comprehension. What we would actually see is a smile. A beaming, joyful smile. For we would realize that this is "the day of His gladness of heart."

There is no greater joy than to discover that God is in an infinitely good mood. Even in the midst of seeing His people stuck in the lies of the wilderness, the joy and gladness of God is still beaming. The Psalmist rightfully declares, "He who sits in the heavens laughs" (Ps. 2:4). Why such laughter? It is not because the Lord doesn't mourn with those who mourn or feel the pain of those who are suffering in the earth. No, the Lord in His love completely identifies with us in our pain and is near to the broken-hearted. But His nearness and mourning is not one of depression and weakness. It is that of tender mercy and of drawing near to His children. Nonetheless, the overarching theme of His heart is one of triumphant confidence and joy. And He invites us to see this joy and be strengthened by it.

God is not anxious over the state of the world and the destiny of His church. We need to know this. God is not wringing his hands, worried about the plans of kings and emperors and dictators. And guess what? God is not even anxious over whether or not the church will mobilize enough energy and efforts and prayers to fight away the evil. He is not fretting and wondering if Satan is going to somehow win in the end. How could he, when Christ is already revealed as the complete victor? God is confident and radiant, beloved reader. He is happy. Another Psalm tells us that He is more joyful than *all His companions* (see Ps. 45:7). Why is this? Because He has the highest and clearest vision of us all. He sees the finished work of His Son and the union that has already been accomplished. He knows that we are "coming up" out of our dry and deceived places.

The revelation of a happy, joyful, and confident God is probably one of the healthiest truths a person could renew their mind with. Depressing and violent wars are fought in the name of angry and sad gods. Church services filled with depressed and anxious people are often the result of those same people staring into the mirror of a joyless, sorrowful god. We become the god we worship, hence the murderous fruit of the crusades and jihads that begin with those who have a deceived understanding of God's face.

Of course, those are extreme examples. But the same thing happens in a more subtle way throughout the world of everyday Christendom. It is easy to point the finger at the extremists, but the real problem often lies in the church buildings and homes where people look up to God and are deeply unsure as to His disposition. Is He smiling upon them, or is He angry and waiting on high to punish? This uncertainty produces a wide array of insecurities in the hearts of many saints. And insecurity produces a wide array of terrible fruit.

The prophet Isaiah said that the Lord waits on high to be gracious to us (see Isa. 30:18). He is actually longing to bestow kindness and mercy upon our hearts and lives. This is His position and His disposition—warmth, kindness, and grace. Health and joy come to the person who knows that this is the truth about God. They know that they are His beloved and that His face is ever shining (even in the midst of our weaknesses and in the worries of a violent wilderness). We have so often fashioned God into our own hurting and depressed images, using an unenlightened interpretation of the Scriptures (particularly the law) to try to back up our depressed and angry god. But once again, the words of David ring truer and deeper than any deceptive doctrine:

...In Your presence is fullness of joy...
(Psalm 16:11)

Why is He filled with joy and why is He smiling towards us? It all goes back to the crimson seat. The Lord has made "purification of sins and sat down." The Mercy Seat stands firm. His Son's work was far more effective and more powerful than the work of Adam and the mess that he left behind. Religion would like to exalt the work of Adam above Christ, but this is just theological dust in the wind. Soon it will pass into a distant memory as the light of eternity dawns.

Perhaps the dust of the religious "city" and its misinterpretations of God's heart is getting into your own eye. Perhaps you do not fully see the truths being unveiled here as you look out at the church's procession through history. But I would encourage you then to continue to gaze. Look longer and deeper at that glorious Mercy Seat and its triumphant King. The mighty cherubim themselves look down at the Mercy Seat and gaze into the wonders of its meaning. These are "things into which angels *long* to look" (1 Pet. 1:12).

As we gaze into the wonders of the blood splattered on the Mercy Seat, joy springs free in our hearts. Wisdom and revelation begin to flow. We realize that we are seated with our heavenly Bridegroom and we are moving in triumphal procession. And this procession is not just any other procession. It is a "wedding procession" that is sealed by the blood on the sedan seat. Jesus has cleansed us and united us to Himself—and *He does not believe in divorce*. The journey we're on is one of complete confidence, intimacy and love. Nothing more and nothing less. The wilderness will only fade as we behold the light of this wondrous truth.

14 Our Present Union

Go forth, O daughters of Zion
And gaze on King Solomon with the crown
With which his mother has crowned him
On the day of his wedding
And on the day of his gladness of heart.
(3:11)

This portion of the Song had begun with a question: "What is this coming up from the wilderness?" As we gazed with the Daughters of Zion we saw that it was something beyond description... *This*, this is Christ the King.

But it is not only Christ the King. It is His travelling marriage caravan. This is the King seen on the day of His wedding, the hour of joy and union. At the very end of this section, our gaze reached its sharpest focus. We saw the King and realized what everything was all about. The unveiling of Moses's tabernacle and thousands of years of religious history came into the light with a simple stroke of the pen in the hands of Solomon. The mercy seat, the wilderness tabernacle, and our own journey towards a full life in Christ—everything ultimately points to the reality of covenantal marriage and love.

With that being said, we need to now address something of extreme importance before moving forward in our journey. Let's take a moment to explore our *present union* with the Lord...

The Year of Jubilee

The Song says that this is the "day of His wedding" and "the day of His gladness of heart." This is a time of complete jubilee and it distinctly connects to the biblical "Year of Jubilee" (see Lev. 25). Every fifty years in ancient Israel, Hebrews would celebrate a special year where prisoners would be released and property would be restored to its original owners. Debts would also be cancelled. This Year of Jubilee would have been a highly anticipated and celebrated time amongst God's people. Yet it always pointed to something greater.

When Jesus began His ministry on the earth, He started by announcing His entire purpose in coming into the world. This announcement came in Jesus's first sermon where He quoted from the book of Isaiah. He said that He came to proclaim the favorable year of the Lord, the day when captives would be set free and those in bondage would be released (see Luke 4). It is a passage that directly relates to the Year of Jubilee, which would be fulfilled though Christ's coming.

The Year of Jubilee, which was meant to be a time of great gladness for God's people, pointed to Christ's work of redemption—and to the gladness God would also receive through it. In His redeeming work, God's property (mankind) was restored to its true Owner by the ransom payment of Christ's blood. Mankind, who was in prison to ignorance and deception, was given release through Jesus's death and resurrection. Our debt to the law was also cancelled. We know now that it was "for the joy set before Him" that Christ endured the cross (Heb. 12:2). So it could also be said that it was for "the gladness of His heart" that He endured being crucified. What was this joy and gladness? This was the joy of redeeming us so that we would be re-married to the Lord in a new and everlasting covenant.

All along, everything was about a wedding day when the two would become one again. This was the purpose of Christ's coming and it is the highest meaning of Jubilee. No one can now take the Lord's joy away from Him, for His joy has been made fully complete at the cross. Though we do not see this all manifested, He knows the end from the beginning. And it is His desire that we would share His joy and know this same complete gladness as well.

But now I come to You; and these things I speak in the world so that they may have My joy made full in themselves.
(Jn. 17:13)

The day of gladness has already come. We are *now* in the Year of Jubilee. For those with eyes to see, this is the day and year of the Lord's re-union with mankind. And it is actually a greater and more complete union than what Adam and Eve originally enjoyed in the Garden.

So if it has not been clearly understood yet, allow me to clarify what we are getting at here, even though this could be a controversial statement for some...

We are not "engaged" to the Lord.

We are *already* married to Him because of His work on the cross.

Already Done

This might be quite obvious and redundant for some. But for others this might challenge our entire understanding of our present relationship with the Lord. Therefore, a deeper look into this subject is warranted.

Think about it. In the natural realm, marriage is designed to be consummated by blood when a virgin bride unites herself to her husband. The consummation of our marriage with the Lord occurred when we were united to Him in His death and blood was shed on the cross (see Rom. 6:5). Like Eve coming forth from Adam's side, Christ's Bride came out of His own wounded side. The cross was truly the place where the covenant of marriage was cut. This is absolutely essential to understand.

The night before Jesus was going to be crucified, He told His disciples that He was going "to prepare a place" for us. This is often connected with a Jewish bridegroom who would go and prepare a physical home for his bride where they would enter into on their wedding day. Many Christians over the centuries have built interpretations of that passage from a wilderness perspective, saying that this "place" is some mansion prepared in heaven that we will go to when we die. But the word "mansion" in John 14:2 is actually a poor translation added by the old English translators that does not correlate with the word's original meaning. That word simply means an abiding or dwelling place. It is the same word used for "abode" when Jesus later says, "If anyone loves Me, he will keep My word; and My Father will love him, and We will come to him and make Our *abode* with him" (Jn. 14:23).

Jesus was not talking about going home and building gold mansions for us. Jesus was going to the cross and leaving for three days that he might prepare a place for us *in the heart of the Father*. He said, "In *that day* you will know that I am in the Father, and you in Me, and I in you" (Jn. 14:20). He was speaking of the day of His resurrection when this union would be fully revealed. He was going to lead us back to God and bring us complete access to the Father. That's why when Jesus said that He was preparing a place for us, He followed those with words with: "I am the way, and the truth, and the life; no one comes *to the Father* but through Me" (Jn. 14:6).

After His resurrection, the apostles began to preach that we now have access to the Father because of the work of Christ (see Eph. 2:18). This is the place He prepared—union and intimacy with our Abba—and it is our greatest reward that we can begin enjoying right here on planet earth. For the fiftieth time, "eternal life is to know God" (Jn. 17:3). Yes, there are wondrous things to anticipate when we cross over into the next age, where our *eternal life* will extend even further. But we can begin to enjoy our married life with the Lord right now!

So when Paul tells husbands to love their wives like Christ loves the church, he is drawing a direct parallel to Christ and us (see Eph. 5). Christ is our Husband and we are His Bride. When Paul told the Corinthians that he "betrothed" them to one Husband, he was referring to the fact that he actually led them to the Lord in the first place (see 2 Cor. 11:2). The word for betrothed can simply be translated as "join together." Now I understand that this marriage will be fully manifested and celebrated in the days to come and that a feast will be shared as the full Bride comes together. That is why it is a wedding *procession*. More and more people are awakening to this gift and receiving this amazing love along the way and there is a great and final celebration ahead. But the coming feast is the "supper of the Lamb" (Rev. 19:9), which involves feasting on something that already happened—the sacrifice of the Lamb of God.

I am not just mincing words here or playing with semantics. It's very important we understand this, for this issue gets at the root of this book and the root of the awakening that is coming upon the Body of Christ. A fiancé cannot have the intimacy with her bridegroom that we are called to have with ours. Furthermore, a fiancé does not yet share her future husband's name. We are only able to pray and speak in the Lord's name because we have taken His name as a bride takes her husband's. We now have access to everything Jesus has in the same way a married woman has joint access to her husband's household. The awakened Bride understands this and embraces this. Her prayers flow like a river and her declarations come forth with the confidence of a woman who knows that she is made one with her husband.

In the "engaged" mindset, all the church knows is longing and delay. Like the sleeping Shulammite, she sits on her bed and searches diligently for her loved one but only finds him in occasional encounters. Like a Hebrew woman might occasionally bump into her promised fiancé, this mindset does not allow for the permanent oneness of His presence. Our prayers also lack the confidence that comes with the knowledge of a sealed union. As a result, the Shulammite does not encounter a complete joy nor she does she have a quenched thirst—two things that Jesus promised to us in the here and now in John 15:11 and John 4:14 (and many other places).

The church, behind her wall, has refused to see this finished work and has thus relegated the wedding day of a completed covenant of union to some far off point in the future. But this is a paradigm shift that the Lord is bringing to His church. As you've probably begun to see, this revelation lays the foundation of the Song. It is the growing and recurring beat that sets its eternal tempo.

We are now awakening to a wedding day that has already occurred and a Year of Jubilee in which we already stand. We are in the day of God's gladness and are invited into the wedding celebration even now. This wedding procession is certainly leading towards an incredible time of manifestation and victory, perhaps right in the natural city of Jerusalem. But the language of the church has become so future-oriented that it keeps us from enjoying what we have in the present moment. So God is taking us from longing to satisfaction, where we overflow like a fountain through our present union with Christ.

I understand that there is a necessary longing to see more of the Kingdom manifest on the earth, but it will most clearly appear through a people who are enjoying and embracing that Kingdom right now. We may long to know our Bridegroom more, but that longing should never begin from a position of lack. We are fully united with the Lord and we can explore more of the riches of our inheritance in Christ every day. This is an adventurous life of intimacy and exploration. We are no longer beggars longing for more of God in weeping sorrow. We are the secure Bride who is invited to enjoy and take hold of her Bridegroom with boldness and joy. We can certainly rejoice in the expectation that the future will only get brighter as the King and His host make their victorious march forward. But we can rejoice now, knowing that we are seated with Christ in that momentous march.

So with that, let's turn our eyes back to the travelling marriage seat as it makes it procession through the wilderness. There is a breathtaking mystery unfolding before our eyes. You see, the Lord has descended into our wilderness and united Himself with us through the incarnation. When God became man, He was becoming one with us in our wilderness of sin and our perceived separation and lack. The marriage actually took place in the wilderness of Golgotha, the place of the skull. This is where Jesus cried out "*I do*" in complete and final wedding vows. The mercy seat was splattered with blood and the covenant was eternally established. We were redeemed in that moment and this covenant cannot be undone.

Though we still appear to be in the wilderness, we are "coming up" out of it as we awake to the glory of this new covenant. We are now coming into the awareness of a glory that we have already been given *in Christ*. So with fresh eyes let's read Paul's words again:

But thanks be to God, who always leads us in triumphal procession
__in Christ__ and through us spreads everywhere the fragrance
of the knowledge of him.
(2 Cor. 2:14 NIV).

Second Selah

There are times to pause, meditate and soak in the wonders of God's love. Those are important *Selahs* that we should take often and spontaneously as we make our journey with the Shulammite. But there are also times to pause and take a *Selah* for others reasons, one of which is to look and reflect on certain things that may be keeping us back from embracing what the Shulammite's journey is revealing...

If you have come this far in the book, you have come across some pretty radical claims as to the *present* power and reality of the Gospel. We have a tendency to struggle with such claims when we do not see it all manifesting in our lives or in the overall church. But more than the lack of visible evidence, a good part of our struggle involves deep-seated thoughts with theological roots (often passed down from our denominations and traditions), which reject what is currently available to us in Christ. As a result, there is a watering down of the current realities of the Gospel that we are called to experience.

As an example, many people will acknowledge and talk about a "legal union" with God that was accomplished at the cross. They will recognize that a union has taken place, but that this is only a "positional" reality which holds no strong and tangible evidence in your present life (unless of course *you* do a bunch of lifelong spiritual jumping jacks...but really, the full weight of this union along with its consequences and benefits won't be enacted upon your life until you die and get to heaven, or until *the day* of Jesus's return). These "legal" and "positional" truths are often spoken dryly and plainly as nice theological facts that are more of a side-note to our spiritual journey.

I want you to pause and soak in the fact that your "legal union" on the cross is far more relevant and present than you could ever imagine. You are united to Christ not in some philosophical sense, but in a real and tangible way. Do not let people dry up the joy of the Gospel with words like "legal" or "positional." Do not let others extinguish your expectations of the wonders of Christ's power and redemption. As long as union—or holiness or victory—is some "positional" truth, it can remain in a *position* high up in heaven beyond your reach in the land of theological discussion or allusive future hope. It becomes something nice to talk about instead of something that you can grasp onto and expect to impact you right now.

This is what happened time and time again in the nation of Israel when they forgot the wonders of God's delivering power at the Red Sea. They settled into a status quo religion, instead of trusting in God's sea-splitting power to fall afresh in their everyday lives. Like the cross in our own day, the story of the Red Sea had become a nice conceptual memory instead of a reminder of the present power and majesty of God. (You might imagine thousands of Hebrews making Red Sea emblems for their necklaces and "celebrating" the event once a month while life carried on as usual.)

I could not let this type of thinking go by without at least bringing a quick challenge to it in another pause and meditation. Obviously, there are whole books that address these issues and a few paragraphs are almost laughable to a person who is steeped in these kinds of theological discussions. But this is not the time for a debate. Besides, many debates are more about heart issues than they are about the actual Scriptures being tossed back and forth. It often comes down to whether or not a person is truly open to the full wonders of Christ's salvation.

It's kind of like the atheist who is closed in their heart towards God. As long their heart is closed, they will try to use nature to find evidence against God's existence (and they may be satisfied in their minds regarding their *natural* evidence). But if their heart is open, they will find nature quite easily illuminates them to the truth of a Creator. In the same way, if a Christian's heart is resistant to some of these issues then they can find all the Scriptures they want to argue against these things (and they may be quite satisfied with their *Scriptural* evidence). But if their heart is open, they will find illumination from the Word accordingly. Both nature and Scripture declare the glory of God in their own unique ways, but both can be misinterpreted depending upon the heart of the observer.

It's time to recover a wondrous delight in all that the Gospel provides. It's time to take these things from beyond just "positional" and "legal" to active and present. If we don't, we may find ourselves carrying these mindsets as a load on our backs. Then, instead of being co-companions with the Shulammite, we will become a distant observer and critic as we watch her travel further into the Promised Land of union with Christ while we stay on the sidelines arguing over words and concepts.

The realities that the Shulammite is encountering may be difficult to believe, but as long as her heart is open God can do wondrous things—even beyond what she could ask for or imagine.

15 The Shulammite's Perfection

How beautiful you are, my darling,
How beautiful you are!
Your eyes are like doves behind your veil;
Your hair is like a flock of goats
That have descended from Mount Gilead
Your teeth are like a flock of newly shorn ewes
Which have come up from their washing
All of which bear twins
And not one among them has lost her young
(4:1-2)

We are nearing the crescendo of this first part of the Song. Sounds from eternity have rushed towards us, knocking at our ears and asking permission to move down into our hearts. Light has begun to break in like a blast of morning sun coming through cracked and crooked blinds. And now, arriving in the middle of Solomon's poem, we are reaching a climax as the Lord unveils His heart in an even deeper way. It is here that the sound and light intensifies and brings us into a stronger confrontation with the Lord's love for us—and the truths of who we are.

It begins by the Lord once more calling the Shulammite beautiful. Knowing that the weight of this word has not yet fully penetrated her heart, He says it twice. And after speaking it twice, He starts to unfold the reasons as to why He says so. It might be good to take a moment and recall the beginnings of the Shulammite's journey. At the onset of everything, she began by looking for true life and true rest. Though she may not have expected it to come this way, the Lord is leading her there by showing her who she is and what He accomplished and revealed at the cross. He does not want her to see herself through the eyes of her brothers, or the watchmen of the city, or the daughters of Jerusalem. He simply wants her to know who she is, as communicated by the One who cannot and would not lie.

We would do well to ask the Lord for an abundance of grace to allow the following words from the fourth chapter of this Song to penetrate us in a more personal way. May these words step into our souls, into the dwelling place of our hearts, and find a place to lay their head...

Perfect Beauty

As we move forward, there is something that will be important to remember. The following words are not confined to feminine beauty. When the Lord calls us "beautiful" it could be compared to a number of things. When you stand in a vast valley and look up at a high and sprawling mountain range, you might rightfully say, "That is beautiful." When you look at an impoverished child sharing his bread with another, you might also say, "That is beautiful." When a man returns from war and sees his young daughter for the first time in years, their embrace could be described as "beautiful."

There are certain things in life that pass into our vision where we have no other description but *pure beauty*. So too, when the Lord looks at you and the whole church—the fullness of who we truly are—He rightfully says, "That is *beautiful*." Something that is beautiful stands out and touches the heart, emanating something of another world. It carries a completeness to it. Like God looking at His creation for the first time, you can look at something that is beautiful and say that it is "very good" and complete.

With that in mind, the Lord will move on from here to describe seven different aspects of the church's beauty. Throughout the Scriptures, seven is the number of perfection and completion. It was on the seventh day that God rested from His labors, because creation was "finished." *Behold, it was very good.* So it is here that God is declaring our complete and finished perfection.

The seventh day of the week, the Sabbath, was never meant to be about a religious day off to rest our physical bodies. That is a healthy thing to do of course, but the Sabbath was ultimately about a celebration of a finished work. And so when we enter into "the Sabbath rest of God" (Heb. 4:9), we are resting in the finished work of Jesus. God is now fully satisfied in who we are and He calls us to know that same satisfaction as well. He knows that our design and beauty has been redeemed and that the DNA of His Son resides in us. Though ignorance and deception may get in the way of us seeing and experiencing this, God is resting in the truth and calls us to rest in it as well. There is no darkness that can overcome Christ in us from being the final word concerning our lives and destiny.

All of this flows from the revelation found in the wine, the apple tree, the table, the vineyards of Engedi, and all the other elements that spoke of the Lord's death and sacrifice throughout the Song of the Lamb. On the cross, Jesus took away every blemish and imperfection—every "missing of the mark" in our identity as image-bearers—and He destroyed it completely. His body completely bore our cursed life and carried it off into a final and complete death. Now He calls the church (and us individually) to enter into a Sabbath rest. Behold, *we* are now very good. The resurrection of springtime is all that remains, and the grave is a distant memory.

*For by one offering **He has perfected for all time**
those who are sanctified.
(Heb. 10:14)*

The King issues His call of awakening once more by declaring the Shulammite's perfection and giving a seven-faceted description of the beauty that He sees. The following is not flattery. It is not the Lord trying to lift our spirits by speaking some subtle words of encouragement. He is not voicing potential, far-off hopes of what we might be ten thousand years in the future. The following words come straight from the heart of the Eternal, and they bear more substance and validity than the laws of physics. Heaven and earth may pass away. The hills and forests may dissipate; the very atmosphere surrounding our planet may shrivel up and evaporate, but His Word will not pass away. And that Word includes the following...

1...Dove's Eyes

"Your eyes behind your veil are like doves," He begins.

Earlier, the Daughters of Zion were invited to look into the face of God, the face of the King traveling in victorious procession. Now the King looks back at His Bride and returns the adoration and awe. He will begin with the centerpiece of her face—her eyes—and compare them again to doves, which is a symbol of the Holy Spirit. In Revelation 5:6, the Spirit is described as being the very eyes of God. And so here, Jesus is saying we too have the eyes of God.

There is nothing like realizing that we have our Father's eyes. There is no greater sense of purpose and belonging than to know you resemble and look like your Heavenly Dad. We are not orphans circling the dust of this planet hoping to find a place to belong. We are the sons and daughters of a glad and happy God. We look like Him. We resemble Him. As we look into His face we find that we are staring into the mirror of our family origin.

There are great stories and fairy tales that pour out of the heart of mankind like water, ever speaking the truth of the Gospel. One such story involves a baby princess stolen from her parents by an evil witch and raised to believe she is a servant and swine (and in some cases made to believe she is the witch's daughter). Her life is filled with a haze of depression and gloom, which is all the more painful when she looks into her heart and knows that she is made for so much more. But the bright and glad day comes when through a series of amazing circumstances she finds out the truth. She is not a servant nor is she the daughter of a miserable witch. Rather, she is royalty. She comes a great line of kings and queens who have reigned valiantly and justly. Though she may have believed otherwise (and such belief would cast a dark cloud over her mind), the truth begins to break in. And as it breaks in, she realizes that she has a glorious inheritance that was hidden from her eyes...

Such is the glory of the Gospel, and the joy that comes when we realize we look like our Dad.

Spiritually speaking, eyesight relates to perspective, revelation, and focus. Having dove's eyes means that we can see our life and the world around us from the Holy Spirit's perspective. We can see with clarity and grace. Our vision is fixed and steadfast just as a literal dove has narrow tunnel vision that only looks in one direction. When we see people, we do not focus on their problems but rather their destiny. When we look at difficult circumstances, we only see a greater opportunity for God's glory to shine through. When we look at the calamities of this world, we see the sovereign, resurrected Lord and the destiny of the whole earth being filled with knowledge of the glory of God. There is a heavenly perspective in the Lord's eyes that refuses to focus on darkness and problems.

The Lord is looking at her here and saying that she has the same ability as her Father to maintain a heavenly vision and focus. Those eyes are already there—she only needs to realize it. Though the walls and sleep are still somewhat present (as we will especially see in the next chapter of the Song), the Lord looks beyond that. He speaks through the veil and declares that she has 20/20 vision. He doesn't even acknowledge her spiritual sleepiness here. He sees only her true identity and destiny.

I believe part of the reason Jesus is beginning with the eyes is because He wants to purify our confidence in "seeing." He wants us to know that we have the ability to see and perceive truth. If we do not realize we have dove's eyes, we will be tempted to doubt that we can even comprehend the truths being spoken in this Song. Thankfully, our marred focus and depressed perspectives were also carried into the grave of Christ's death. Our pessimistic, religious viewpoints were drowned in the flood of His blood. Impure vision was crucified. Even the power of doubt was defeated at Calvary, and it is now Christ's faith that abides within us.

So let this first facet of our beauty ignite your faith and help you realize that you have the ability to see clearly. When your perspective feels corrupt and when your vision has been filled with filth, take a refreshing drink of Song of Songs chapter four, verse one. Remember that you have pure eyes, and that darkness cannot overcome that purity. You resemble your Father who is a great, strong, and focused King. As the old expression goes, your eyes are the windows to your soul. And so when the Lord looks through your window He sees the Dove hidden within—the very life and Spirit of your Father.

2...Goats of Gilead

Next the Lord speaks of her hair, comparing it to a flock of goats coming down from the mountain of Gilead. As we continue to see the symbolism and parables hidden in the Scriptures, this verse also brings great illumination and hope as to who we are and what we are capable of. Hair in Scriptures very often speaks of wisdom. We do not have the time to extrapolate all the reasons for this symbolism, so I would encourage you to pray into and research these things on your own. A good starting place in regards to hair would be the Proverbs, which makes several references to hair (especially gray hair) as a sign of wisdom.

So here the Lord is speaking to the *wisdom* that flows from her like a flock of goats would appear to be flowing down the rocky mountainside of Gilead. There is a *flow*, a naturalness to her wisdom that the Lord is seeing. This teaches us that God's children were designed to have His wisdom flowing within them. And one who walks in that wisdom absolutely captures and moves the heart of God. Now Gilead means "rocky regions" or the "region of the rock." Our spiritual ears should perk up at the word "rock," for that is a direct symbol of Christ and His work, as mentioned earlier. Therefore, the backdrop of all our wisdom is the work of Christ, like the backdrop of the flock of goats is the rocky terrain of Mt. Gilead. Indeed, Christ is Wisdom itself (see 1 Cor. 1:29), and to know Him and His finished work is to walk upon the terrain of complete wisdom and knowledge.

Interestingly, scholars also believe that the word Gilead could mean "the hill of testimony." It was on the hill of Calvary that the testimony of our righteousness and forgiveness was established. To walk in the word of that testimony—our righteousness in Christ—is to walk in the greatest flow of wisdom possible. This is also why Jeremiah mentions the "the balm of Gilead" (Jer. 8:22), which speaks of the Lord's healing balm that comes from the salvation Jesus accomplished on Calvary's hill.

Another aspect to this analogy is the reality that a person who had a flock of goats would find their sustenance from those animals. A person's flock provided them with regular income and was one of the most important parts of their life. So too, to walk in the wisdom of Christ is to find a regular income of riches and sustenance. As many of the Proverbs declare, wisdom is indeed true gold and silver. There is nothing greater and more prosperous than to discover the wisdom of Christ within and to allow that wisdom to guide our lives. The King is pointing out this incredible wisdom that He sees within the Shulammite, calling her to embrace it herself and walk it out. As the Shulammite comes alive to Christ within, this wisdom will move into flowing action.

Let me also add here that many commentators would point out that hair could represent a person's dedication. This is in connection to the Nazirite vow in the Old Testament, where a sign of one's dedication to the Lord was to let their hair grow without cutting it. There are layers upon layers of truth to the Scriptures, and much can be gained from seeing this aspect of her hair as well. Suffice it to say that a person's unwavering dedication to the Hill of the Testimony, and to the Lord who was crucified there, is nothing but pure beauty and delight in the eyes of God.

3...Sheep Newly Washed

The next aspect of her beauty that the Lord highlights is her teeth, which He compares to freshly shorn and washed sheep, all of which "bear twins and not one among them has lost their young." The teeth are a symbol of understanding, for it is with the teeth that one chews on something given to it and puts into a form that can be swallowed and digested. It is with our spiritual "teeth," so to speak, that we chew upon the meat of the Word to the point that we are able to receive it into our hearts and walk it out. Somebody can simply hear the Word, but Jesus said it is those who hear *and understand* the Word who bear an abundance of fruit in their lives (see Mat. 13:23).

So the Lord is calling out her ability to understand the things of the Word. Not only is there a Spirit of revelation (eyes) and wisdom (hair) within her, but there is also the Spirit of understanding (see Isaiah 11:2). This is the God-given ability to process and tangibly walk out what she has seen and learned so far. This understanding is compared to clean, white sheep that have been shorn and washed. When a flock of sheep is shorn, all of the sheep look pure and uniform. Thus there is a unity and purity to her understanding. She is not divided and wavering upon the tossing waves of different doctrines and ideas. Non-essential or inhibiting doctrines and excess have been shorn—or cut off. Her understanding is simplified and rooted in Christ.

This understanding in Christ is also washed in the waters of His death. "Being washed" speaks of our immersion into the death of Christ. When one receives wisdom or guidance from the Word, it is so important that we understand that our sin has been washed away. All hindrances to obedience have been dealt a deathblow at the cross and it is no longer in our nature to go against God's direction. However, if we still believe that we are dark sinners (like the Shulammite believed in the beginning of the Song), it will be difficult to obey and follow the Word. For we will obey out of the place of law instead of a trust that the Word is already in us (1 Jn. 2:14). It is now part of our very nature to obey God.

If I am running the danger of speaking too generally and theologically, let me make this practical and give an example of what is being said here. Let's say that the wisdom and guidance the Lord is speaking to you involves loving and honoring your spouse in a deeper and more sacrificial way (or your parents, or your boss, or the poor...you can fill in the blanks). If you believe that you are "selfish" at heart (in other words, you think you still have an uncircumcised heart), your double-mindedness about yourself will lead to double-minded behavior. You will be selfish some days and somewhat selfless on others, and your obedience to the Word will come in slow starts and stops. But as you "shear" and cut off the teachings that say you are a wretched sinner with an inward propensity towards sin, and as you wash yourself in the knowledge that you are a holy child of God, it will become easier to obey. In fact, it will become natural. For it will come from the truth of your heart. So again, as our understanding is unified in Christ and washed in the knowledge that our sins were crucified and removed, we are able to digest and obey his wisdom.

Digestion and obedience always lead to fruitfulness. The "sheep" of her teeth all "bear their young," which comes out multiplied. Or, in other words, as "twins." So there is a multiplication of fruit that comes from this pure understanding. Again, those who hear and understand are those who bear multiplied fruit in their lives—"some a hundredfold, some sixty, and some thirty" (Mat. 13:23). Furthermore, the Lord says, "Not one among them has lost their young." This is important to note as well, for Jesus said we would bear fruit and *our fruit would remain* (Jn. 15:16).

When our understanding is united and washed in the work of Christ, there is an obedience and a fruitfulness that remains! Glory to Jesus Christ! There is such wondrous fruit to taste in our walk with God. This is the fruit of seeing other people experience freedom and joy in Jesus. It's the fruit of deep and satisfying relationships, and that of sacrificial love that helps others find their way in life. This is the fruit of peace and joy that overrides every other contradicting emotion. It is the fruit of abounding provision and protection. All of this is fruit that comes out multiplied and then sticks around permanently. All because of who we are in God's sight...

16 The Mother of All the Living

Your lips are like a scarlet thread
And your mouth is lovely
Your temples are like a slice of a pomegranate
Behind your veil
Your neck is like the tower of David
Built with rows of stones on which stand a thousand shields
All the round shields of the mighty men
Your two breasts are like two fawns, twins of a gazelle
Which feed among the lilies
(4:3-4)

When the Lord God introduced Adam to his wife for the first time, Adam tasted a satisfaction that he had not encountered before. God had given him a longing for a partner with whom he could equally share life together, one who would reflect his own life in a way that the rest of creation wouldn't. When Adam beheld his new bride, his joy and satisfaction could not be expressed in plain language. So he went on to utter the first piece of Hebraic poetry found in the Scriptures. This was in Genesis 2 when Adam declared that Eve was "bone of his bone and flesh of his flesh" (Gen. 2:23). He saw his own reflection mirrored in Eve and was in awe over the uniqueness of her beauty.

It is astonishing to find that all of this pointed to something much greater in the heart of God. All along it would be Jesus who would stand in awe over His Bride, the church, and would declare that we too are bone of His bone and flesh of His flesh (see Eph. 5:30 KJV). A satisfaction and joy would come upon Him as well and He would also use poetry to communicate His heart. Jesus is looking at the Shulammite in this part of the Song and is totally satisfied in seeing His image and likeness mirrored in a unique partner. One with whom He will get to share the Mystery of God's life. This satisfaction, or good pleasure, brings an explosion of words that cannot be said plainly, for they arise from a place of wonder and celebration. And so in His complete contentment, the King continues to poetically declare the perfections He sees in His redeemed life partner.

He will also begin to speak of the calling and destiny within her...

4...The Scarlet Thread

"Your lips are like a scarlet thread," He continues. "And your mouth is lovely."

Christ looks at the Shulammite and sees the loveliness of her mouth, which symbolically includes her words and speech. This loveliness is specified because her lips resemble and speak of the "scarlet thread," a reference to the book of Joshua. In order to understand this reference, we will need to turn there and take a look at the story.

In Joshua 2, there were two spies from the Israelite army who went to survey the city of Jericho before it fell. There they met a prostitute named Rahab who received the spies into her home. Upon helping them escape Jericho, she asked that her and her family would be spared from the destruction coming upon the city. One simple piece of instruction was then given for her and her family to be spared. If she were to hang a scarlet thread from her window, the Lord and the Israelite army would pass over that house in the hour of judgment. Everyone inside the home would be saved.

It was a strange request, but it worked. The sinful prostitute was indeed saved from the judgment upon Jericho solely because a scarlet thread was hung from her window. This is a similar picture to the one found in the Passover story on the night that the angel of death came to bring judgment upon Egypt. The Hebrew people were told that if they were to put the blood of a lamb upon their doorposts that the angel would pass over them. They were obedient to this strange request and while the rest of the city experienced death and destruction, those who had the blood on their doors were spared.

The scarlet thread is of course the revelation of Christ's blood. It was not the righteousness of the Israelites inside their homes that saved them from the angel of death—rather their salvation came because of the blood on the doorposts. Similarly, it was the scarlet thread that saved Rahab and her family. Where judgment and destruction come upon sin, there is a hiding place of mercy in the shelter of Christ's wounds. There we are found completely righteous and accepted by God. He sees the blood of His Son and it is as though sin and spiritual prostitution did not even exist in our lives. We are fully embraced as innocent and pure.

"Out of the abundance of the heart, the mouth speaks," Jesus once said (Mat. 12:34 NKJV). When one's heart is filled with the knowledge of Christ's work and the wonder of His grace, the mouth will speak forth this truth. And when one's lips are speaking and declaring Christ and His mercy, there is a sweetness to the breath that the Lord absolutely loves and enjoys. Unfortunately, there are many believers who utter words that either subtly or blatantly reject the truth of the scarlet thread. This reveals that the contents of their heart still hold a sense of guilt and sin consciousness. In their prayers, conversations, and self-talk they mutter words of self-loathing and doubt.

You can hear this especially in the prayer meetings at multitudes of churches. Many people's prayer lives consist of beating themselves up, talking about how horrible of a sinner they are, and the lack of holiness they possess in the sight of God. They ask for mercy over and over again, not recognizing that the fullness of mercy and grace was totally and finally poured out. This, my friends, is like bad breath spewed out into the face of God. Nobody wants to be near someone who has horrendous breath—and to speak such faithless prayers, which reject our righteousness in Him, is to release that kind of breath to heaven.

The prayer that is spoken in agreement with Christ's work is different. This is a prayer that is lovely to the Lord and pleasing in His sight. One who engages in self-talk that agrees with the love and encouragement of the King in this Song has a mouth that is full of fragrance and life. It is like a *scarlet thread*. This goes beyond prayer and self-talk as well. It also involves our speech towards other people, especially those who are lost. The beautiful church is one who speaks of Christ's mercy and finished work to the nations and draws others into the shelter of God's conquering love.

Like the phrase "all roads lead to Rome," one could say, "All Scripture leads to Christ." This commentary on the Song of Songs might appear to some as overly Christocentric, but that is indeed what the Word is all about. He *is* the Word. Jesus is both the milk and meat, the Alpha and the Omega, and the cornerstone and the capstone. Everything comes from Him and flows back to Him. So once again we find the Lamb hidden in this Song; the scarlet thread that runs throughout the whole Bible. The person whose heart and mouth are filled with this truth bring great pleasure to the Lord. Our breath and lips are pleasing in His sight, for we acknowledge the eternally sweet-smelling aroma of His Son's sacrifice.

There is nothing we can do in our own efforts to somehow please God. God is pleased by the work of His Son alone. And so the lips that simply agree and say yes to that work bring an effortless pleasure to God. It is like having the finest scarlet thread hanging constantly from the doorpost of our hearts.

5... *Pomegranate Seeds*

Next are the "temples," which is a word that refers to the Shulammite's cheeks. The King is looking at what surrounds her lips and mouth and sees something that He compares to a slice of pomegranate. Now there are two things that stand out when one slices open this delicious fruit. First and foremost is its color, which is the same without and within—crimson. The second thing one would notice is that individual seeds are strewn throughout the fruit. The symbolism of each element then is quite rich. Like the scarlet thread, a connection to the color red emerges once more. The color carries the same meaning of Christ's blood. The dispersed seeds then are the sparks and carriers of the DNA of that fruit. They represent the seeds within us that carry and multiply the message and life of Christ.

Consequently, the progression from the lips and mouth makes perfect sense. That which surrounds her speech (whether it's the speech involved in prayer, regular conversation, or the teaching and sharing of the Gospel) are the seeds of redemption. Her mouth is lovely and its contents hold the seeds of true life. As she speaks (or just shines forth the beauty of her face—her full identity), there are miracle-working seeds that are spread across the earth. In all who see her and receive her words, there is a harvest of multiplied beauty and fruit.

It is here that the Lord is preparing the Shulammite to see her identity as one who is a releaser of life and fruitfulness in the earth. She is the one who carries the crimson seeds of His redemption. Therefore, we will bring our attention back to Eve, the wife of Adam. Just as Adam was a foreshadow of Christ, Eve was a foreshadow of the church. Jesus is called the "Last Adam" (1 Cor. 15) and the church is called the "wife of the Lamb" (Rev. 19). Hopefully, this has already been made clear enough.

The church is the fulfillment of what Eve represents. In ancient cultures, a person's name spoke to their identity and destiny and Eve received her name from her husband accordingly. She was named "Eve" because she would be "the mother of all the living" (Gen. 3:20). But now it is Jesus's partner, the Shulammite, who is the fulfillment of this calling. She is to be the "mother" of all true life on the earth. She carries the seed of her Bridegroom and is destined to release and birth that eternal seed wherever she goes. This is the seed drenched in crimson, the Word of the cross. We partner with Jesus to freely and joyfully scatter the seeds of new life wherever we go.

So far, much of this book has focused on the Shulammite's awakening to her perfection and to the unfailing love of her Lord. This is something that must come first before she is to awaken others. For how can we bring rest to the weary and life to the dead when we ourselves feel dead and weary? David appropriately prayed in the Psalms, "Restore to me the joy of your salvation and sustain me with a willing spirit. *Then* I will teach transgressors your ways, and sinners will be converted to you" (Ps. 51:112-13). As we wake up to the joy of the Gospel, we will then be empowered to effectively release its message across the earth.

The first part of this Song is then more about the Shulammite coming back to the full joy of her salvation. Later on, however, she will be released into leading others to that place of life and rest as well. We are not there yet, but it is important to note that the Lord is beginning to speak of her destiny as the true Mother of All the Living. Where there is barrenness and death, the rising church is the one who will reverse it by the Spirit of grace. Like a mother carrying the joy of new life into the world through labor, the church is called to release rivers of life into dry and desolate places out of her own innermost being. Though this calling is not fully revealed until later in the Song, its truth will continue to build in this chapter, especially as this section closes up with the description of her "breasts"—the ancient symbol of nourishment to the young. We will dive into this much more, but we must continue on with the immediate words at hand. We will turn next to the description of her neck.

6...*The Tower of the Mighty Men*

To put it quite simply, the neck is the part of us that connects the head to the body. It is the covered bridge through which the train of the spine delivers messages and direction to the rest of our physical being. It is also the vehicle by which we keep our heads locked and steadfast in one direction. It can be compared to stubbornness or pride (as in being *stiff-necked*), or in the positive sense, to perseverance and determination.

The Shulammite's neck is compared to King David's armory, a tower that was filled with the weapons and shields of the mighty men. King David is the greatest warrior in the Scriptures and his mighty men are perhaps some of the most fierce, valiant, and relentless men who have ever lived. They were victorious wherever they went and were unflinching in the face of danger and opposition.

If your lips bring forth the word of Christ's blood and release the seed of His life, you will need a strong "neck" to stand firm when opposition comes. The Lord is encouraging the Shulammite to know that He already sees this firmness and dedication within her. There is a spirit of perseverance woven into her very being. Whether she sees it herself or not at this point is irrelevant. The point is that God sees it. And what God sees and believes is firm and settled. Faith is simply the effortless agreement and awareness of what God already knows to be true. Faith does not strive to create something, it simply sees what God sees and lives accordingly. In this part of the Song, the truth is revealed—a fierce strength and perseverance lies within us. It is a steadfastness that will endure whatever comes our way. It is a perseverance that can press through 1000 enemies just as the mighty men did on numerous occasions. This is the strength that lies within us and it is part of the breathtaking beauty that Christ sees in His church.

As far as the neck connecting the head to the body, we also find here that the Lord is speaking of the church's steadfast ability to flow with His headship and leadership. Just as the mighty men followed King David's orders with bravery and haste, the church has what it takes to follow the orders of our King Jesus. We are united to His wisdom and direction the way a body is united to the direction of the brain. We have the "mind of Christ" as well as the necessary equipment to be led by that mind (1 Cor. 2:16).

Multitudes of people throughout Christian communities talk about the importance of church unity. Many are often devising plans and trying to figure out how to make this happen. But there is only way for a physical body to work in unity, and it's quite simple: Remain attached to a healthy brain! A working brain orders the body to function in unison just fine (without the help of the body parts figuring out things on their own). So too, our connection to the Head, Jesus Christ, will bring forth effortless unity as a church body. It's great to have church-unity events and ecumenical services and initiatives. However, if people are not learning about their intimate connection to the Head, it won't mean much in the long run. We will go on devising our own plans and efforts at accomplishing church unity, instead of resting in the Mind and Presence of Christ.

Thankfully, the ability to rest in that union with the Head lies in the veins of every member of the church throughout the earth. In fact, it's not only the ability to stay connected with the Head, but it's an overcoming, victorious and *persistent* ability to stay connected. This is an ability compared to David's tower, which was filled with shields of strength and protection. This ability is within us and has always been there. We only need to hear and understand this truth. (And, praise God, we have the "eyes" and "teeth" to do this!)

7...Two Fawns

Next He compares her breasts to two fawns, "twins of a gazelle that feed among the lilies." Both in and outside of the Scriptures, breasts are an ancient symbol of nourishment to the spiritually young and immature. This speaks of the milk of the Word that we feed to those who need to grow in their own journey of love and awakening. Jesus is declaring that the Shulammite has the nature and ability to not only speak and release life to others (in conquering strength), but to also follow-up with pure nourishment and edification. Again, "twins" speaks of fruitful multiplication. There is a multiplying fruitfulness in her nourishment to others. In other words, as she nourishes the spiritually young, those being nourished will go on to do the same to others. Life will create more life!

The church's destiny is not solely to release and awaken the life of Christ on the earth through the Holy Spirit. It is also to mother and nurture that life as it comes forth. This speaks of a word that has been quite tarnished and stained over the past few decades, but is nonetheless a key part of our inheritance in Christ. That word is "discipleship." As the Mother of All the Living, the church is anointed to nurture and disciple *whole nations* (Mat. 28:19). Humanity is stunted in their growth and the Shulammite has the ability within her to go forth and bring humanity into maturity, into the full stature of Christ who is the original blueprint for mankind.

Now when we bring up discipleship we are not talking about boring meetings where people are asked probing questions and often leave feeling guilty or carrying a to-do list (or perhaps just filled some new head knowledge of memory verses). What we are talking about here is the multiplication of Jesus's organic life in one another. This is a multiplication that "feeds among the lilies." Remember that the "lily" spoke of our identity earlier and it further revealed the Lord's tender love for us. True discipleship leads others to feed on God's love and on the knowledge of our true nature in Him.

Jesus, in His physical body on the earth, modeled this for His corporate body, the church. He multiplied His own life in the twelve apostles and they went on to multiply that life (through the delicious pomegranate seed) in their own disciples after them. Jesus symbolically spoke of this reality when he broke and multiplied the five pieces of bread and fed masses of people with it.

159

Jesus said that the bread was a symbol of His very life and nature. After multiplying and feeding others with this bread of life, there were twelve baskets of that same bread left over. All of this points to true discipleship. Jesus would multiply His life in the twelve apostles and they would feed the nations with that same inner life. This cycle of life and multiplication would continue in each heart that awoke to the message of grace and union.

Like a mother feeding her infant, there is an intimate and caring bond that is also tied into discipleship. Discipleship is rooted in mothering and fathering. It is relational and it is about living life with people, just as Jesus also demonstrated. The apostle Paul explained to one of his planted churches that he was like a gentle mother and a strong father to them (see 1 Thes. 2:7, 11). Discipleship was not seen as a program or a task-list. Instead, it involved family life and centered on the message of union with Christ in His death and resurrection.

So Jesus is encouraging His church to see their gracious and natural ability to nourish and build up the young. Again, this ability is hidden within all of us. We do not have to be experts in Bible knowledge or disciplined coaches and taskmasters. We simply need to enjoy His own life within and share it freely with those around us. As we do, we will lovingly and tenderly care for others who the Holy Spirit draws under our wings. As fathers, we will build them up, discipline, and encourage them, and as mothers we will nurture and care for them. This will naturally bring forth *twins that feed among the lilies.*

Divine DNA

We are neck-deep in symbolism and metaphor at this point and I hope I haven't lost you in the midst of it. Let me clarify with some very basic language for a moment what we have seen so far. Jesus is declaring what He sees in His people, in each one of us individually and in the whole corporate church. He sees that we truly have a heavenly vision and perspective, the eyes of God.

We have a wisdom and a dedication that flows from the Rock of Christ's salvation. We have a spirit of understanding that is able to digest truth. As we digest His truth, we are obedient to His Word and bear much fruit in our lives.

We are then a people whose mouth and lips declare His finished work and whose cheeks are chock-full of seeds that carry the power of that same message. There is a spirit of perseverance in us to stand firm in that calling—and to stay connected to Jesus as our Head. And we not only have the ability to release life, but to then nourish and water that seed and build people up in their salvation. We have it within us to steadfastly edify those who are spiritually young. This is woven into all of us.

We may not be fully manifesting these realities, but be sure of one thing. Within a frail and tender infant lies the entire DNA coding of a strong adult. A baby may not appear to have the ability to walk or run, but it is there nonetheless. A baby has everything in it that will one day lead him or her to do great things. It is the same with us. We were knit together in the womb of the Holy Spirit and were given everything we needed for life and godliness. We were then taken out of Christ, just as the Woman was taken out of Man. We have left our earthly "parents" of a flesh-based existence and have come into the truth of our new birth in Christ's resurrection. We are now one spirit and one flesh with God. We are perfectly united to Him and will stand and shine as the Mother of All the Living— which is all by His grace and His Spirit.

As we ourselves simply feed upon the milk of Christ's kindness and salvation, we will naturally and effortlessly grow into the stature that is already within us. And as we learn to stand firm in that stature, we will have the grace to help others feed on Christ in the same way. This will produce a worldwide harvest among the nations, the harvest of the life of Christ. It will be the hope of glory—Christ in us—coming forth.

17 Rotten Pomegranates

Your temples are like a slice of a pomegranate
Behind your veil
(4:3b)

Before moving forward with the King's words and the Shulammite's destiny, I want to briefly stop and deal with a traditional interpretation of the cheeks and pomegranates. Like the fig tree element earlier in the book, this is a little bit of a side road on our journey, but it will connect quite succinctly with the rest of the Song. In fact, it will help us see the main path more clearly when we return to it.

First, let me tell you about a house...one that is old and decrepit and ready to fall apart. Many believers try to make their home in this house, but it's not ideal. The electricity and the heat come and go. The leaks in the ceiling are many. A stench of urine and animal dander hangs over the carpet like an invisible blanket, and slight holes in the walls bring an unwelcome waft of the outside elements. Yet still, many try to make this into a home and even believe that this is what it's supposed to look like. Maybe their mansion in heaven will be better one day, but for now this is the home they believe they must accept.

The house I am referring to is an old model of Christianity and it comes out in many commentaries on the Song of Songs, particularly in their interpretations of the pomegranates. This is an interpretation that speaks to something much bigger than can be fully addressed in this book. Nonetheless, we need to at least touch on it; otherwise it has the potential to be an elephant in the room that is quite distracting from the truths at hand. We're going over beautiful words of love and life, but if this elephant is not called out, your mind might be divided and you may not hear everything else being said.

The elephant I am referring to—and the "old house" interpretation of this verse—relates to false humility and shame. It has to do with a Christianity that praises self-deprecation and fear and makes confidence out to be something of the devil. It is a "beat-myself-up" Christianity, and it's growing staler and more decrepit by the minute (even though many stewards of the old house are trying to patch it up with the duct tape of control and the rusty nails of fear). Accordingly, in some translations, teachers and commentators will say that the Bride's cheeks are red like pomegranates because she is blushing with shame before God. She is very aware of her sin and this is somehow beautiful in God's sight.

Now if her cheeks are blushing with true meekness and humility that is absolutely wonderful. Meekness is an awareness of one's strength and power, but you are able to keep it under control with dignity and respect. Humility is then simply the act of agreeing with God and thinking little of yourself. Not little in the sense of having low self-esteem. Little in the sense that your heart is so filled with the love of the Lord and love for others that you are free from constantly worrying and focusing on yourself. This kind of humility and meekness is a valid interpretation of the pomegranates. But many commentaries go farther than true meekness and humility and talk about one who is ashamed of their sins and who holds a sense of unworthiness in God's presence.

This exaltation of unworthiness and false humility runs like a dirty gray thread throughout church history. We might think of the reformer Martin Luther before he got a revelation of grace, when he climbed up stairs on his hands and knees in order to earn

God's favor and show remorse over his sin. This was a pattern of behavior and thought that was prevalent throughout centuries of Christendom. It goes all the way back to the early church where zealous preachers called Judaizers would begin to legalistically influence the church's thinking. They would impose extreme regulations upon the believer's body if they were to be truly accepted before God. In others terms, they wanted the saints to beat themselves up to earn justification and peace with God. But Paul called these preachers "mutilators of the flesh" (see Phi. 3:2).

Unfortunately, we are more apt to focus on the obvious abuses of this kind of thinking while missing some of the more subtle versions of it. For instance, most believers today will cringe at the thought of people in the Middle Ages walking around whipping their own backs in order to express humility and penance before God. But then many of these same believers will internally whip themselves in their prayer lives, as mentioned in the last chapter. As a result, many walk around in a subtle self-loathing and fear and oddly consider this to be holy. Depression and low self-esteem reign quite easily in many believers' hearts, often because such feelings are completely unchallenged by their theology of Christian suffering and humility. This is then reinforced by many teachers who would even cringe at the phrase "self-esteem." To them, that's just modern pop-psycho mumbo jumbo that's irrelevant. They would say *forgot about self-esteem and get on your face before a holy and almighty God* (and they might say this in a really deep voice and quote some Scriptures about picking up your cross in order to make it seem extra anointed and powerful).

Much of the Bride's cheeks are red today, not because they are blushing with meekness, but because they have been slapped by preachers and Christian leaders. What's sad is that these preachers then tell them that they are beautiful in the eyes of God. Their cheeks are like pomegranates, they say. But this is not the redness of face that the Lord looks for. This is the redness of a Bride who has been beat by hireling husbands who have kept her away from the intimacy and grace of Jesus. It is from modern day

Judaizers who look extremely holy with their zeal and knowledge of the Scriptures, but lack the heart of the Bridegroom as seen in this Song.

The True Fear of the Lord

Let's expand this discussion and get a larger look at this elephant. There is something even bigger going on here and it has to do with the phrase "the fear of the Lord." To many people reading this book, they may have felt like its overall themes and messages disregard the fear of the Lord. But there is a wide gap between the true fear and respect of God and what many teachers describe it as. The fear of the Lord is something beyond what any hellfire preacher can conjure up (and their conjuring is not the fear of the Lord anyway; rather it is just human manipulation and control that leaves people with a form of religious anxiety, instead of transformative and exuberant worship). The true fear of the Lord awakens a thrilling awe and worship before a God of glory and power, so much so that it quickens every spiritual bone in your body to life. It makes you fall in love with Him even more. Even the words "reverence" and "awe" fall short of the power of this phrase.

Sadly, when a lot of people talk about the fear of the Lord, they use it in reference to being afraid of God and of walking on eggshells when it comes to their dirty lives of sin and weakness. In this case, your face is blushing because you know you shouldn't be in the presence of such a holy God with such a dirty life. He is the Master of the household and you are the lowly servant. However, if you are bashful in His presence and keep your head down and eyes low, He may throw you some crumbs from His table. You may even be able to sleep inside for a night, instead of out in the shed (until you do something stupid or make a mistake, then it's back to the work shed).

You see, in this line of thinking you see yourself as an orphan and a slave, and not as a beloved son or bride. I understand that these are extreme examples, but the spirit of it is embedded in the doctrines and mindsets of many Christian teachings. This mindset flows from a "wilderness Christianity," the old and decrepit house where shame before God is considered good. You are seen as holy if you beat yourself up, but in reality this is just false humility. It is the old Judaic leaven of mutilating the flesh, which has run rampant throughout much of the Bride's journey in church history. We may not tell people to circumcise their foreskin anymore, but we add plenty of our own little requirements to supplement the sheer gift of grace.

People who cling to this old house will say that those who are outside—those who preach with intensity on the grace and the finished work of Jesus—are just watering down the fear and judgments of the Lord. They would say that such preachers of grace are just giving people watered down milk, while those who preach on the fear of the Lord are giving the real meat. But their false emphasis on fear is not the meat that people need. Instead, its just garbage that grew stale hundreds of years ago, even though many try to keep the flame alive. I do not mean to come against any individual teacher here or to be divisive and negative. I am simply saying that it is high time the children of God awake from the tyranny of religion, which wants us cowering in a corner in shame. This spirit of religion wants to keep Eve in the bushes, while her true Father is calling her out, declaring her to be the Bride of the King, equally yoked, and the Mother of All the Living.

Think of the intimacy between a bride and her husband (in a healthy, happy love relationship). *This* is one of the closest analogies God can find to communicate the kind of relationship He has purchased for us to have. Just take a moment to imagine what that would look like if we truly understood and embraced that analogy. Imagine the giant broom that would sweep over centuries of Christian thought and expression. If we understood this fully, we would not be slaves cowering before our master as we did our chores. We would instead be sitting peacefully at the table with the Lord, co-reigning with Him in His household, and filled with the joy of our salvation.

As a side-note, I know that Jesus used a lot of master/servant analogies. Some people might argue against the preceding words by utilizing some of Jesus's own teachings. But make sure that you read those parables and teachings in the light of the full counsel of the Word. Jesus did not come to purchase slaves, but a Bride. The prodigal son was given a ring of authority and a celebratory party—not a to-do list upon his return. Service certainly happens, but it happens in the way that a bride serves her husband and vice versa. It is a life of rejoicing and freedom, not fearful service and shame. So rejoice, children of God!

Time to Move On

The prophet Hosea clarifies the dichotomy between slavery and freedom in a beautiful way. He prophesies of a day when we will no longer call God "Master," but rather we will know Him as "Husband."

> *Therefore I am now going to allure her;*
> *I will lead her into the wilderness*
> *and speak tenderly to her.*
> *There I will give her back her vineyards,*
> *and will make the Valley of Achor a door of hope.*
> *There she will respond as in the days of her youth,*
> *as in the day she came up out of Egypt.*
> *"In that day," declares the LORD,*
> ***"you will call me 'my husband';***
> ***you will no longer call me 'my master.'***
> *... I will betroth you to me forever;*
> *I will betroth you in righteousness and justice,*
> *in love and compassion.*
> *(Hos. 2:14-16, 19)*

As we said earlier, this covenant of marriage and union was already sealed at the cross. Every time we come to the Table and drink of His cup, we are remembering the merciful covenant of intimacy that we already have. God is no longer our Master. He is our faithful Husband. The greatest shift imaginable occurred at His sacrifice and we get to live in the glory of that shift *now*! The Song of the Lamb is so much more beautiful than we could have ever imagined.

Many of us are still hiding behind the wall of enmity and shame in one form or another. The wall might not be as obvious as it was in Martin Luther's day, but it still exists and tries to worm its way into certain interpretations of the Song of Songs. It is the wall that makes up the barriers surrounding that old and decrepit house. But it's time for us to move out of there. It's time to truly come away, beloved of God...

Let me also mention one last thing. I recognize that there is often a fear associated with moving out of this house. This is because there are dogs who stand at the door, who bark at us and try to keep us back. These are the same "mutilators of the flesh" that we have already discussed. Paul also referred to these zealous leaders as "dogs." These leaders intimidate countless people in an effort to keep them in the old house. However, I want to let you in on a little secret.

Those dogs have a mean bark. But, surprisingly, they have *no teeth.*

Walk past the dogs.

I understand the ferociousness of their bark (with all the fear-based Scriptures to back it up). I understand that they rear up on their hind legs to make themselves look even more intimidating. They will call you rebellious and deceived and will utter words of poison in your attempt to escape their tyranny. They will tell you that there is nothing but hell and lukewarm Christianity outside the gates of their house. But keep walking. Leave that house behind, for right beyond its gates lies an intimacy and peace like you've only hoped for in the inner recesses of your heart. There is a beautiful life ahead of you in the grace of Christ.

So with all of that being said, we will now get back onto the main path. Let's continue to tune in to the ever growing and intensifying words of love and truth pouring forth from our Beloved. It's time to leave fear and shame behind. It's time to rejoice! To say that over and over again is a safeguard for you. So... "Rejoice in the Lord always; again I will say, rejoice!" (Phil. 4:4)

18 Upon the True Mountain

Until the cool of the day
When the shadows flee away,
I will go my way to the mountain of myrrh
And to the hill of frankincense
You are altogether beautiful, my darling,
And there is no blemish in you...
(4:6-7)

Earlier in the Song there was an invitation given by Jesus for the Shulammite to "come away" into His life and freedom. In that invitation, however, we realized that the Bride still had a strong perception of separation. Because of this, she told her Beloved to turn away, saying she would join him at another time. Hopefully you will remember her words well: "Until the cool of the day when the shadows flee away, turn, my beloved, and be like a gazelle or a young stag on the mountains of Bether" (Sgs. 2:3). In other words, *when the day of Your return truly dawns and all the shadows of this world flee away, then I will be ready to join You in Your life of complete freedom and victory. But for now, we are sep-arated (with an unbreakable wall between us). For You are on the mountains of Bether—the mountains of separation.*

This sense of separation was expanded upon when we looked at the Shulammite on her bed and other elements in the Song. Nonetheless, the Lord has continued to reach out to her, even in the midst of her spiritual sleep, and has brought her on a journey of realizing the true union and love that they already share. He went on to describe the fullness of how He sees her in all her redeemed perfection. He also began to declare her destiny and calling.

In light of these things, we will soon come again to Jesus's call for the Shulammite to "come away." Yet right before He issues this call He will first address her earlier words about waiting for the day of His return—the end of the "shadows" and the end of the alleged separation between them. He will make another correction and adjustment to her perception of separation. Instead of being on the mountains of Bether, He will take His stand on a different mountain, a single mountain. This He describes as the mountain of myrrh and the hill of frankincense...

Here is a paraphrase of His response:

You may see darkness and separation between you and I. But even though the full day of manifestation hasn't dawned, and even though the shadows of self-doubt and fear still creep over your mind, I want you to know which mountain I am really on...

It is not the mountain of Bether.

No. I am actually standing on the mountain of myrrh (the symbol of My death). And it is the mountain of frankincense (the symbol of My sweet-smelling intercession and life). It is upon that mountain that I will continue to stand and make My plea to you.

I, My love, am on the Mountain of My Sacrifice and that is where you and I were made one. That is where the wall was forever broken. It does not even exist anymore.

We are forever united as one.

The mountain of myrrh and frankincense speaks of the altar upon which Jesus was crucified once and for all—the hill of Calvary. The scarlet theme of the Lamb's Song continues to resound and Jesus will not relent until the Bride awakens to the fullness of what happened at the cross. Even until the full day dawns and shadows flee away, the truth of this "mountain" will stand eternal and firm and it will forever enable us to leave our wall and come away into the fullness of Christ's grace. He is still calling her to see and trust in this reality.

Like the Shulammite, there are many people who see Jesus Christ standing on a high mountain of separation, holy and almighty and very far from them. They then see themselves a million miles away in their own spiritual development and strength. As a result, they feel they need to drastically change their lives and do a bunch of spiritual things in order to get near to Him and become more like Him. But in the light of such glory and *otherness*, this work of drawing near to Christ and becoming like Him can feel like an impossibly long mountain range to traverse—like mountains of Bether. So we're often left saying, "*Maybe when the day of His return dawns and the shadows of fear go away, things will change. But for now the life of Christ is far and distant.*" We can hope for occasional moments in His presence, and a victory somewhere in the sweet by-and-by, but our hearts doubt a present and living union with the fullness of Christ.

And yet the full message of the cross is altogether different. It continues to speak to us from another realm. It declares that we are already made like Him and that we cannot get any closer to Him. The rest of His words in this passage of the Song could then be paraphrased as follows:

And so I will say it loud and clear for all creation to hear. You... My disciple, My friend, My church, and My Bride...you are completely beautiful! There is nothing wrong with you. You are perfect, and you are complete. You are without sin in my eyes, for I actually and literally took it all away. We are not separate anymore. Lo, I am with you always, even until the full day dawns.

The night season of this earth may veil these truths from your eyes. The brick-laying shadows of religion may speak otherwise and cause you to stumble and fall and forget who you are. But you are a child of Mine. You are bone of My bone and flesh of My flesh. The myrrh

of My sacrifice and the incense of My intercession have completely removed all distance between us.
    Because of the cross, **you are now altogether lovely.** *And there* **is no blemish in you.**

Song of Solomon 4:7, which effectively and precisely declares our perfection, is a verse that is intricately connected with the rest of the Scriptures. The reality of this verse is indeed the crescendo of Christ's work of redemption on Calvary, which was planned before time itself sprung into motion. In Colossians, which is one of the central books of the Bible that established some of the core orthodox theology of the church throughout history, Paul expresses the same thought as Solomon. Read it carefully...

But now he has reconciled you by Christ's physical body through
death to present you holy in his sight, **without blemish**
and free from accusation.
(Col. 1:22)

Because of the reconciling work of His death on that hill of sweet-smelling incense, we are altogether holy and without blemish. As said before, this is far more than just a *hopeful* or *positional* thought. This is as sure as God's Word. We are now holy *in His sight*...and that is all that really matters. This is not about what is in your own sight when you look at yourself. Or what is in the sight of your pastor, or your parents, or your friends. Or what is in the sight of the rest of the church, including those you may admire and respect. I am talking about how God sees you—and how He sees His church. Because of the myrrh sacrifice of the Messiah, you are holy and without stain. This is a mystery—something that transcends the rational mind and yet stands perfectly and solidly true. Even when sin and darkness appear to be in your life, you are miraculously free from any possible accusation. The truth and the truth alone is a completeness of beauty that cannot be threatened by any accusing voice or temporal experience.

What is happening here, beloved reader, is that the Lord is continuing to liberate the Shulammite from the "dark" mindset and the Kedar self-image, breaking its hold on her with the tenderness of His love and the great authority of His voice. A voice that shatters the mighty oaks and births the heavens and the earth. So much of her journey in this first part of the Song links back to her initial doubts and fears. All along it has been about the Word of Truth penetrating her soul and breaking those fears. The mystery of His grace and His finished work on Calvary is the "knowledge of God" to which the Shepherd has been leading her. She has been caught up in lies throughout her life, just as the church throughout history has been caught up in lies, leaving multitudes with the feeling of being intrinsically "bad." But these things have met their end in Christ. In His resurrected life we are revealed as innocent and whole.

God's voice and love have come to the Shulammite—and to all of us—in the form of Jesus, the most beautiful One to ever grace this planet. He is the perfect representation of the Father's love, and He has revealed the God whom nobody before him had truly seen or understood (Jn. 1:18 & 6:46). Not Moses, not Elijah, not even David or John the Baptist. Everyone else saw the backside of God's glory, like Moses in Exodus 33. But Jesus came to reveal His very face.

And so He has come with the smiling face of God, filled with grace and truth. He is seeing His Bride in the captivity of darkness, surrounded by the wall of enmity. Likewise, He sees her wrapped up in the burdens of the Pharisees and the condemnation of the devil. These things have created a poor self-image that wraps itself around her mind like an iron turban. An image that speaks of darkness and inadequacy and of constantly missing the mark. In other words, the Good Shepherd has seen the Shulammite and His church still living in a "sin consciousness." And so He shouts to her from the true mountain of Calvary in order to break this kind of thinking—*yes, even before the day dawns and the shadows flee away.*

Leaving the Brazen Altar

Though we have covered this issue many times throughout the Song, we cannot quickly leave it. For it is here that we find the purpose of Jesus's shed blood. This is a crowning note in the Lamb's Song and a major undercurrent in Solomon's book. From the start, the Bride has sought after the Most Holy Place—the Eden life of love and freedom. But we slowly found that she has been stuck outside that place, standing at the Brazen Altar, which still speaks of sinfulness and imperfection. Let me explain this a little bit further...

In both Moses's tabernacle and Solomon's temple, there was an altar outside the Holy Place and the Most Holy Place where the people would daily bring sacrifices to atone for their sins (see Ex. 27:1-5). This Brazen Altar formed yet another barrier between them and a sustained rest in God's presence. As long as that Brazen Altar was standing, the way into God's constant acceptance and presence was shut off. Instead, there was a system set in place so that people could clean themselves up day in and day out while never arriving at a clean conscience and a pure identity. God was indeed the focus of this system, but the people's hearts were wrapped up in the system itself, not its focus.

Today we do not bring animals before God, but we do often bring an awareness of our sin in our relationship to Him. Day in and day out, we can also adhere to different systems of cleaning ourselves up in order to become holy. We offer up the sacrifices of prayers and subtle forms of medieval penance to atone for our sins. Because of this mindset, we so often find ourselves falling short of abiding in the constant forgiveness and embrace of the Father. As a result, the issue of *sin* becomes the core topic of our sermons and spiritual conversations. The whole Christian life often gets summed up in messages on overcoming sin and becoming a better Christian. As a result, the emphasis is more on self than Christ. (I understand these are generalities about the church, but take a few months and visit many of the congregations across the world and listen to the content of the sermons and the follow-up conversations and see whether or not this generality is at least somewhat appropriate.)

The language of "it is finished" and "you are *now* altogether lovely and complete" is foreign to many believers' ears. In fact, if a pastor doesn't preach on *sin* then he is often accused of watering down the Word. But what is really getting watered down is the message that you are perfected and sanctified by Christ's blood and that God is no longer counting your sins against you. This is the message that truly convicts and sets people free from different sins in their lives. But when we water this down, Christianity becomes a journey of constantly cleaning one's self up instead of enjoying and resting in the fact that Jesus already washed us clean—once and for all.

The blood came to take away *all* sin consciousness. This was something that the blood of goats and bulls could never do. Something that religion, self-effort and performance could not accomplish either (as demonstrated by thousands of years of failed Hebraic history). A wall of religion was built up, but intimacy was never truly attained. Doctrines and systems were duly established, but freedom never arrived. Only temporary blessing and sustained judgment. A rollercoaster of emotion and spirituality. A burning under the sun.

From the mountain of myrrh, Jesus continues to make His declaration to His sin-focused church. His words "it is finished" resound even deeper. Salvation has come and Christianity is about waking up to what He has already accomplished. As mentioned earlier, myrrh was used in burial preparations, specifically in the embalming of a deceased body. Therefore, its scent is meant to hit our hearts and remind us that our old selves are dead and buried. Out of this restful revelation, there is an overflow of natural fruit and good works that come forth. We are not striving towards the Most Holy Place; we are already seated there in Christ, having died to our old existence. Out of the joy of being freely seated in that place of new life, we manifest an abundance of outward freedom and love.

If we are to truly answer our Beloved's call, we need to set our gaze once and for all on the mountain of myrrh and simply breath in its fragrance and celebrate its scent.

Pure, Pure Grace

Before we close this section, let's address one stumbling block that many people encounter in receiving the truths that flow out of Calvary. This is something that the Jewish people ran into when Jesus walked the earth. At one point during His ministry, the burdened and spiritually enslaved people of Judea approached Jesus with a question. This question involved something with which they were very familiar—*work*. They asked Jesus, "What shall we *do*, so that we may work the works of God" (Jn. 6:28).

Now work was always in the forefront of their minds. They might have been redeemed from Egyptian slavery hundreds of years prior, but the slavery of the law was still alive and well. This is the same root question that pops up today when people wonder if there are conditions to grace. What's the catch? What must we *do* with this message of radical grace and love? How do we *ascend* the mountain of myrrh?

Let's look at Jesus's revolutionary response to the Jewish people. It is the same answer He would give to us today...

"This is the work of God, that you believe in Him whom He has sent."
(Jn. 6:29)

Now this must have been incredibly offensive to Jewish ears at the time. Not just because He was claiming to be sent from God, but because His to-do list was so radically different from the religious system they had built their whole life upon. The one work they were required to do was to simply believe in Him! That was it. This is the revelation that Jesus already ascended the mountain for us. He already seated us in the Holy of Holies! The call is to merely hear and trust this good news.

And so here is the stumbling block. We all want to know our responsibility in the matter; however, when everything is put back on Christ, it makes people nervous. They fear that the message of pure and unconditional grace will make us lazy and give us an excuse to do nothing. So they add a little law and fear into it so that people won't just sit around and "do nothing." What they do not realize, however, is that giving people God's commandments as a *law* to follow is actually hindering their spiritual progress. People end up being "burnt out" and not living in true righteousness and joy. Now of course, there might be people who appear to be following God's standards under a legal mindset, but this is often motivated by fear or by pleasing their pastor or Christian community. The motivation of love and celebration is often absent. And eventually this will manifest itself in gossip, backbiting, lust, division, and all other kinds of fruit that we find running rampant throughout many congregations in the world.

The message of pure and radical grace has always been scary for the church. It feels *too free* and seems too good to say it as plainly as we're doing now. So there are many people who want to run ahead of its offensive stand-alone truth and put red tape around it. We set up new barriers and fences that look a little bit prettier than the iron fence of Moses's law—but they are still fences. They still communicate a sense of condition to grace with slight rules and systems that must be adhered to if grace is to properly be released.

True Freedom

Here's a question we need to consider: *Why did Jesus set us free?*

Thankfully, the answer is straightforward and it's found right in the book of Galatians. For the sake of freedom alone, that is why Christ came. In other words, He came to set us free...so we could be free! He did not come to enlist us as workers or to simply forgive us so we could be given a to-do list or a new legal code to live up to. He came simply because He is good and He desired His creation to be free. He loved us. And he knew that in the pure freedom of redeemed innocence we would live as we are supposed to live.

Pharaoh was once confronted with this call to freedom and accused it as coming from a place of laziness (and the voice of Pharaoh continues to speak through many a preacher today). You may remember that Moses approached Pharaoh and demanded that he let God's people go so that they could take a "three days' journey" to sacrifice to God (see Ex. 5:3). This was another sign and pointer to Jesus's final sacrifice when He was three days in the ground. It is a picture of God calling His people out of bondage into the celebration of Christ's sacrifice. In fact, Moses tells Pharaoh to release the people simply so that they may "celebrate a feast" (Ex. 5:1). Unfortunately, Pharaoh responds in this way:

*But the king of Egypt said to them, "Moses and Aaron, why do you draw the people **away from their work? Get back to your labors!**" Again Pharaoh said, "Look, the people of the land are now many, and you would have them cease from their labors!" So the same day Pharaoh commanded the taskmasters over the people and their foremen, saying, "You are no longer to give the people straw to make brick as previously; let them go and gather straw for themselves. But the quota of bricks which they were making previously, you shall impose on them; you are not to reduce any of it. **Because they are lazy, therefore they cry out,** 'Let us go and sacrifice to our God.'*
(Ex. 5:4-8)

Pharaoh then reinforced his accusation even after Moses continued to implore him to let the people go...

*But he said, "You are lazy, very lazy; therefore you say, 'Let us go and sacrifice to the LORD.' **So go now and work**..."*
(Ex. 5:17-18a)

Pharaoh called this a redemption for the sake of laziness. The apostle Paul called it freedom for the sake of freedom. Saying that Christ did it all may ignite some anger in certain taskmasters who will claim it is just a message of laziness that neglects personal responsibility. But like Moses, we can never back away from the call of freedom—the offense and scandal of grace.

It was for freedom that Christ set us free; therefore keep standing firm and do not be subject again to a yoke of slavery.
(Gal. 5:1)

Now listen very carefully. There is *much* fruitful work that will come out of the life that is overflowing in the revelation of grace. But it will always be *fruit*. The work is not the seed itself nor is it the root. The Word of grace is the seed and the root system is a growing trust in His love. These are the ingredients that make up a fruitful life. These are the trees that grow by the rivers of God.

This revelation of grace might be also compared to a sunrise that erupted over a beautiful ocean when all humanity was lost on the dark shores of self-works and sin. The sheer gift of this sunrise invites us to stare into its light and it calls us to explore an endless ocean of holiness and peace. But it is a special sunrise. It is a sunrise that lifts the heart and carries you into the sea all by itself. As you simply turn away from the distractions of the shore and stand in awe at the sun, change begins to take place quite effortlessly. There is certainly an ocean of exploration and adventure with plenty to *do*. But so many of us need to just stop, take a breath, and stare into the sun as it envelops our soul.

There are well-intentioned shepherds—sons of our mother, the watchmen of the city—who want to make sure we're busy "doing" what we should be doing. They do not want us to go overboard with the message of God's freely given acceptance and righteousness. But we do need to go completely overboard! We need to jump off the ship of self-works and dive fully and completely into the grace of God that was manifested at Calvary.

Paul himself made this very clear to his own disciples when he left them in charge of shepherding one of the most significant cities in the ancient world. In his final speech to the Ephesian leaders, Paul said:

> *And now I commend you **to God and to the word of His grace**, which is able to build you up and to give you the inheritance among all those who are sanctified.*
> *(Acts 20:32)*

Notice that it is "the word of His grace" that builds you up and *gives you* your inheritance in Christ. You don't give yourself your inheritance (i.e. the Holy Spirit's presence and power, good works, life everlasting). Grace gives you your inheritance. So we are called to simply cling to the Word of grace. This is also why Paul asked the Galatians if they received the power and presence of the Holy Spirit by adhering to the law or *by hearing the Word with faith* (see Gal. 3:2). All we are to do is receive and celebrate something that is already true. This is in fact the stumbling block for many people who are dead-set on working and *doing*.

I know this may seem like another rabbit-trail from the Song of Songs, but I assure you it is not. The Shulammite's journey throughout church history has run into this issue over and over again. The church has built its towers of Babel in an effort to add to the salvation of Christ and His finished work on Calvary. But at the mountain of Zion—the mountain of myrrh and frankincense—only one thing is needed...

To simply *be*.

To sit as His feet in peace and receive His word of kindness and acceptance. To stand still and enjoy our salvation.

Fortunately, this message of grace is progressively being restored to the church ever since she fell away into legalism and into man's forms and control. But even still there are many amongst the Bride who still need to hear its sweet tune and tap into its unconditional beauty and grace.

You are saved, you are free, you are perfect...apart from what you do.

Here in the Song of the Ages, the Bridegroom is singing over His Bride and He is speaking these unfathomable truths. Many other voices would like to come in and complicate it and add a bunch of red tape around it. But His words remain pure and matchless.

I just love you.
And you are perfectly beautiful. Period.
You are made holy because of My blood—because of all that I have shown you thus far. Whether or not you are far into the ocean of a holy life, it is true nonetheless.
Stand in awe of it... Be still and behold the salvation of your God... Rest.
For these are the green pastures you seek. This is the life that you and all humanity are looking for. A life of complete acceptance. A life of complete freedom from burdens, guilt, and fear. A life of being loved simply for who you are.
And, as you've seen, who you are is more than you could possibly imagine...

Christ is not on the mountain of separation. There is no distance between us and His promises of freedom and new life. He has gone to the mountain of myrrh and frankincense, and there His sacrifice continually speaks of a perfect redemption and a scandalously free gift of grace.

There is nothing left to do than to just *believe*.

19 The Summit of Truth

Come with me from Lebanon, my bride,
May you come with me from Lebanon
Journey down from the summit of Amana
From the summit of Senir and Hermon
(4:8a)

When a cloud becomes heavy with moisture and can no longer contain its growing weight, that moisture begins to overflow and drops of water fall to the earth. Sometimes it's only a few drops and sometimes it's a lot. In the passing pages of this Song, we find a brilliant white cloud forming over the heart and mind of the Shulammite. The Lord Himself is filling this cloud with heavenly water as He speaks more and more words of love and truth to her soul. He has spoken so much and He will continue to speak. Yet as He does, that cloud will soon burst. A flood will come like never before. And it is that breaking point that we are approaching in these final portions of our text—a point that will forever change the Shulammite's journey.

The Lord has completely reversed her perception concerning the "mountains of separation." He has called her to gaze on the glory of free and everlasting grace, once again affirming her union with Him at Calvary—the mountain of myrrh and frankincense. As He said before, He will now say again: "Come away, my beloved!"

His call and His desire for her has not changed. He still longs that she would be fully awake to the new life that He has given her. His desire (think about that, the very *desire* and yearning of God) is that she would experience all the fruitfulness that flows from receiving His wondrous love.

In this fourth chapter of Solomon's Song, the Lord begins His second call to "come away" with slightly different words. He is now calling her attention to Lebanon, which lay to the north of Canaan and bordered the Promised Land. Right on the outskirts of this land was Mount Hermon (also known as Mount Senir) and the Amana Mountain, which was the source of a great river that flowed in the north. Many English translations will make the assumption that the Hebrew text is calling the Shulammite to *leave* Lebanon and these mountains. But the Hebrew could actually be translated as Solomon asking her to "look down" from these mountain summits (and thus to see from their perspective). "Look down" and "journey down" could be translated the same way and so varying commentators and translators will interchange the terminology. This is an important distinction if we are to understand the full meaning of this second call to "come away."

What we will end up discovering is that both translations—both *looking* down from the summit or making her *journey* down from it—carry remarkable meaning and will bring great illumination to our hearts. His Word is truly a lamp unto our feet and a light unto our path. It fills our hearts with the oil of faith and it guides our paths even before the day dawns and the shadows flee away. This is a portion of His Word that is filled with an abundance of oil and light.

And so the path has been set before us and the smell of rain hovers above. Let's look more closely then at His luminous Word.

The Summit of Amana

The word "Amana" is bursting with symbolism and meaning. It is no accident that the Holy Spirit moved Solomon to pen his poetry by calling the Shulammite to look down from this particular mountain. The word "Amana" primarily means "truth." Part of its root meaning actually comes from the Hebrew word for "Amen" or "so be it."

From the very beginning of this Song, the King has released eternal truth within the Shulammite's soul. Over her eyes lay a veil where she saw herself in darkness and saw the Lord as being far out in the distance. Her skin had been burnt and the realities of pain and separation were the filter through which she has understood her relationship with God. But the King has begun to change these perceptions as He leads her to drink from the fountain of His completed sacrifice. He also brought her beyond the limitations of man's religions and doctrines. It is now here that He calls her to finally take her stand on everything He has shown her. He is calling her to the summit of all Truth where she can finally shout, "Amen!"

To put it another way, the Shulammite is being led to a joyful and simple agreement with the heart of God where she can lay down and say, "So be it! I believe!" Everything the Lord has said thus far has all pointed to this summit, which speaks of a pinnacle of reality that is higher than everything else. The "truths" of this world all fade thousands of miles below this particular crest. The words communicated by her mother's sons, by the world system, and by the devil himself all become a shadowy whisper in the light of this summit. Above everything else—every difficult circumstance, every mistake of her own, and every wounding of her past—the truth stands firm. This is perhaps why the Psalmist said, "Forever, O Lord, Your word is settled in heaven" (Ps. 119:89).

Anyone who has climbed to the peak of a mountain and looked at the view below can tell you how different things appear from that perspective. One could be walking amongst a maze of streets and cities or trails and forests, but upon the mountain that overlooks it all you see the entire landscape with clarity. There is a peace at the summit that eclipses the chaos of life down below. Anyone who has travelled by plane and sat in a window seat can affirm this as well. The terrain of the land, sprawling and vast as it is, becomes quite simple from those heights. This simplicity in the eyes leads to a simplicity in the heart. And that simplicity is the peace we are called to in Christ.

Apart from any works or deeds of her own, the reality of the cross stands firm. This is the glorious stumbling block and offense of the Gospel that we have already covered. While the whole world looks to attain to some mountaintop of their own making, the summit of Truth towers above everything else. At that summit we find that God is madly in love with us—and by our union with Christ in His death and resurrection, we are pure, free, and spotless. All this because we are the "the rose of His heart" (Sgs. 2:1a TPT), the one He absolutely adores. From eternity past, the Father has always known us as His pure children. And far out into the future, He has always looked ahead and saw our unending destiny of purity and love. The momentary blip of sinfulness in our eternal timeline was fully covered in the blood of His Son. We may now receive the title of sons and daughters again, knowing that there is no more darkness in us. We are *His*.

This reality stands above everything.

Looking and Journeying Down

The real mountaintop of Amana in Solomon's day would have most likely given people a rich and full view of Canaan, the Promised Land. This goes for many of the mountain peaks of Lebanon, including Mount Hermon (or "Senir," as the Amorites called it). Therefore, Jesus has truly been helping us to "see" the Land. In other words, He is showing us all that He accomplished in His death and resurrection. Both Amana and Hermon speak to the reality of us seeing the height, length, and depths of our union and redemption in Him.

Psalm 133 particularly speaks of the dew that falls from Mount Hermon when "brothers dwell together in unity." There at the summit of Reality, the place of the cross, we dwell with our Elder Brother, the Lord Jesus, in complete unity. The recognition of this union releases the oil of the Spirit and it leads to the blessings of "life forevermore" (see Psalm 133:1-3). This is the summit of Truth upon which we already abide. For we are *in Christ* and He is *in us*.

The great fallacy of "wilderness Christianity" over the centuries has been this idea of *journeying up* towards some mountaintop through trials and tribulations or through surrendering and suffering. We have majored on these topics and loaded up God's children with impossibly high burdens like the Pharisees did with the Jews. But this is all rooted in self-righteousness. As a result, God's children often feel like such a journey is only for the spiritually elite (some specially called missionary or revivalist who did several 40 day fasts), and many end up living with a sense of disenchantment. The Promised Land becomes a place far out in the distance and many of these believers end up settling for a hope in heaven when they die. Then preachers and leaders go on to call these "settling" Christians lazy "Laodiceans" who need to wake up and get serious.

But this is not how the Lord speaks to His beloved Bride in this Song. He calls her to awaken to the realm of true faith. True faith (Promised Land Christianity) is the reality that our starting place *is* the mountaintop. We already abide there because we are already seated in heavenly places in Christ Jesus (Eph. 2:6). It does not get much higher than that. Every religion in the world, including the religious elements of Christianity, makes a god out of pilgrimage and suffering in hopes of one day reaching nirvana or paradise. It is all about our sweat, blood, and tears.

But the *amana*, the truth, is all about Jesus's sweat, blood, and tears—not our own. In this life of grace and love, we will participate in those tears through the call to love the least of these. Some will even shed their blood by standing firm in their faith in Christ. But we are to never boast in any of these things. At the end of this age, all believers, including the greatest martyrs, will cast their crowns at the feet of Jesus. The church will finally see that it was always about *His* work and *His* blood. Any valid sacrifice on our part was simply the sacrifice of joyful gratitude and wild celebration.

The truth, the *amana*, is that we are already at the finish line right from the beginning of our race. We are already fully embraced and accepted in the love of our Father. There is nothing higher to achieve, no higher mountain to climb than the place of simply being loved and tenderly cared for by our Dad. Thus we are not journeying *up* to victory. Rather we are journeying *from* victory with an "amen" agreement to His unchanging Word. We can look down from this perspective, seated securely with Christ, and move forward confidently. We are to look down in peace and journey forward in triumph. Both phrases work together. Our starting place is the realm of "*it is finished.*"

This also corresponds to the issue of "sanctification." The Scriptures make it clear that we are already sanctified in Christ. The outward "journey" (or process) of sanctification is actually enjoying and discovering more of the gift we already have in Him. In our union with Christ we are already complete and He has become our very sanctification and life (see 1 Cor. 1:30). As we discover Christ within, this manifests outwardly. Once again, this is the great scandal, offense and glory of the Gospel. While everyone else is busy climbing mountains, trying to find what they're looking for in their spiritual or physical lives, the truth is that we already have what we need at the summit of Amana. It is the place of peace, the apple tree under which we find shade, and the green pastures for the sheep.

All along she was already there. It was only different lies and fears that distracted her from its panoramic views. Nonetheless, the kiss of the Spirit has come and it has begun to awaken her to the place of rest and righteousness. It has called her to see the Promised Land of union with Christ.

The Rising Temple

Before mentioning Amana or Hermon, the Lord had first called His Bride to look and journey down from Lebanon, where these mountains stood. It is important to note that Lebanon was the source of the building materials for Solomon's temple. King Solomon, the writer of this Song, would always make sure that the wood for the temple came from the great cedar and fir trees found in the north. In fact, there is a good possibility that the wood used for the temple was taken from the forests surrounding the mountains of Amana and Hermon.

Solomon calls the Shulammite to look and journey down *from Lebanon...* This goes to show that it is from the place of heavenly truth—the summit of His love and perspective—that we find the raw materials to build up God's temple. We have said all along that God's temple is the radiant Shulammite church. As she beholds the glory of God's grace and His finished work at Calvary, the Shulammite (the living temple) will arise and shine. In other words, she will be "built up" and edified by the "fir" wood of the cross. She will shine with the reflection of Christ as she recognizes that she is His mirror image and likeness. And as she shines, kings will be drawn to her brightness. The abundance of the sea and the wealth of nations will come into God's church (see Isa. 60:1-5). This wealth is the very gold of God's image within man, which Jesus came to purchase and redeem.

We have noted before that Solomon was both the builder of the temple and the writer of the Shulammite's journey. These two things continue to go hand in hand. The Lord's desire has always been to raise up a people who would be a holy nation and a royal priesthood in all the earth. A corporate mother carrying God's seed of life to the barren world.

The temple was a physical representation of the purposes within God's heart—that a physical people would hold the very essence of His presence and nature. They would call those in the outer courts to come near to the place of covenantal love and union. The Shulammite is then a poetic representation of the same purpose. She is comprised of a physical people who are one with His very nature and life as well. They too will call those on the outer courts to come near unto the Truth of who Christ is and what He has done. Later on in the Song we will see this reality manifest more clearly.

No Place Like Home

It would be quite fitting at this point to mention another film that communicates some of the things we've been discussing—*The Wizard of Oz*. This is a foundational piece of cinema with a story that is considered timeless and classic. Like many other great stories, it also gives us an allegory of the Song that God is singing over His creation. The elements of the Gospel within this particular film relate to the journey of the lead character Dorothy. She is a young girl who is lost in the Land of Oz and is searching for a Wizard whom she hopes can bring her back to her home. Along the way, Dorothy encounters three characters, and all three are also searching for something of inestimable value.

She first meets the Scarecrow who is hoping to find a "brain," or intelligence. Next, she finds the Tin Man, who is looking for a "heart." Finally, she comes across the Lion who is trying to find "courage." All of these characters end up making a journey to the mysterious Wizard in hopes of him providing what they need. As they move forward, they are worried and fearful about "lions, and tigers, and bears" and other dangers along the way (we'll discuss the Shulammite's own fears in the next chapter, described as "lions and leopards"). Nonetheless, they press through these fears and continue to seek after the Wizard.

Once they do find him, the Wizard tells the four companions to defeat the Wicked Witch and bring back her broom. They are successful in this endeavor, but at the end of the story it turns out that the Wizard that they sought was just smoke and mirrors. He could not deliver on his promises. This can easily be compared to man's religious journey. People go to the bewitchment of religion to try to attain what they feel they are *lacking*. Dorothy's defeat of the Wicked Witch and the exposing of the false Wizard can be likened to the church waking up from this bewitchment. It is when these illusions are broken that Dorothy and her companions find that they already had what they were looking for. In fact, they had these things the whole time—they were just *ignorant* of the truth (or didn't believe it). The Wizard of Oz ends up giving them items that only acknowledge the brain, heart, and courage that was in them the whole time.

But at the center of the story is Dorothy's own revelation. At the end, she is told by the Good Witch Glinda (who is a Holy Spirit type and figure) to simply tap her ruby slippers three times. She is told that by doing this she will be brought to the place she is looking for. This proves to be true and Dorothy discovers that there was never a reason to worry or fear, because the key to home was strapped to her feet the whole time. She ends up awakening from the dreamland of Oz to find herself home-safe with her entire family. Like the Shulammite, she only needed to wake up.

20 Lions and Leopards

...From the dens of lions,
From the mountains of the leopards
(4:8b)

Throughout the Song, there have been key issues that show up in different forms of symbolism. Just as the table, the myrrh, and the apple tree all pointed to Christ's sacrifice, there are also repeating symbols that speak of condemnation, law and fear. If the Shulammite is to look down from the perspective of truth and make her journey from that place, she will need to deal with these issues as they try to intimidate and paralyze her along the way. These are now poetically described as the lions and leopards found in the Lebanese mountains. Previously, it was the wall or the bed, but now it is the leopards and lions that speak to these things. The Lord is still asking her to move past the wall, but He is saying it in a totally new way. He is now calling her to stand on the summit of His Word and let go, once and for all, of fear and condemnation.

The lions and leopards of this Song are not positive symbols. When it's not the Lion of Judah, lions in the Scriptures often represent the enemy who "prowls around like a roaring lion, seeking someone to devour" (1 Pet. 5:8). The meaning of enemy's lion-like roar is unveiled by one of his other names—"the accuser of our brethren" (Rev. 12:10). The enemy's roar consists of accusation and condemnation. Satan is known to use the law against us in order to keep us hiding in the bushes in fear of our Father. He then devours people simply because they are paralyzed in their spiritual identity under the weight of guilt and the feeling of being isolated from God. This is the lion that we are to move past.

The leopard does not show up as often in the Scriptures, but they were nonetheless a common predator in the northern regions of Israel. They are chiefly known for one particular attribute—their dark spots. Jeremiah makes this point when he asks if it is possible for a "leopard to change his spots" (Jer. 13:23). In that context, he is asking if Israel could change their wickedness, and is basically saying that just as a leopard cannot change its spots, so Israel cannot change its wicked heart.

But of course we know that Jeremiah later received a word from the Lord that a new covenant was coming where those wicked "spots" would be taken away. That deceitfully wicked heart would be cleaned up and renewed (Jer. 31:33). This happened at the cross, which obviously leads us back to our "lovely versus dark" discussion. It shows us once again that this whole Song is intertwined with the same message. The leopards then speak of the lie of a false identity and provide further ammunition for the enemy's cursing accusations. It is here that I love to think of the good old King James Version of Song of Solomon 4:7, that eternally deep and glad verse. It says, "Thou art all fair, my love; there is **no spot** in thee." We are spot-free in the eyes of the King, and thus we are to move right past these lying leopards as well.

As one makes their stand on the peak of all truth, and lets the journey of their life flow from that place, they will encounter the lions and leopards of judgment and accusation. These forces try to find legitimacy through an old (already crucified) identity and draw their roaring intimidation from the law. They try to keep up the wall of fear, enmity, and distance in an effort to stop the already victorious church from believing in the glory of God's love and her identity in Christ.

As we said before, the Scriptures are often like a multifaceted diamond with different angles in which to see different truths. Therefore, we could turn the diamond of this whole passage about Lebanon and its mountains and see it from a different perspective. This passage could be looked at as though the Lord is calling His Bride to simply come away from the *northern* regions. This is important, because the north in Scripture is very often connected to judgment, since it is the direction from which many judgments came. Enemy nations were often raised up in the "north" in order to inflict the curse and penalty of the law on God's disobedient people. This revelation and perspective becomes quite powerful when we understand more clearly what the lions and leopards represent...

Saved from Wrath

The only other places in Scripture where lions and leopards are paired together are found in the words of the prophets when they are hurling judgments upon the nation of Israel. Both Jeremiah and Hosea threaten God's punishment, which they compare to lions and leopards that are lying in wait to destroy the city.

> *Therefore **a lion** from the forest will slay them,*
> *A wolf of the deserts will destroy them,*
> ***A leopard** is watching their cities.*
> *Everyone who goes out of them will be torn in pieces,*
> *Because their transgressions are many,*
> *Their apostasies are numerous.*
> *(Jer. 5:7)*

> *So I will be like **a lion** to them;*
> *Like **a leopard** I will lie in wait by the wayside.*
> *(Hos. 13:7)*

Hosea and Jeremiah compared God's judgments to lions and leopards on the prowl. When the people transgressed the law and fell away from God, enemy nations and other destroying forces would come and ravage the people of Israel. The prophets attributed all of these things directly to God, but they are actually the dark forces that steal, kill, and destroy when the people moved out of the boundary of His law. Before the Messiah came to deal with sin once and for all, God gave the law partly for the purpose of protecting people from the full consequences of sin. If they obeyed the law fully, they would remain in a life of complete blessing (which, of course, was impossible to do). If they disobeyed the law, they would then subject themselves to a curse of destruction and evil. The "lion and leopard" prophecies about the consequences of people's sin are then speaking about demonic forces of destruction that would be unleashed upon the people and the city.

Trust me, God is not the one breaking into Jerusalem and slaughtering babies and raping women. He is not sitting on His throne trying to manipulate matter into a virus that can inflict the most intense pain and suffering in the people who catch it. There was an old covenant perspective of God's sovereignty that attributed every single action to Him (and unfortunately, many still cling to this perspective). But the lions and leopards were really the demonic forces behind Babylon and other invading armies and forms of judgment.

When the people left the boundary fence of the law, God repeatedly warned that they would encounter these forces. But God was never the One who would murder people when judgment came upon the nation. He was actually trying to protect them in the midst of their sin. God is the Author of life. Satan is the one who holds the power of death (see Heb. 2:14). Jesus came to make it very clear that Satan is the murderer, not God (see Jn. 10:10). Yet it was when the people of God disregarded the protective boundary of the law, that they made themselves susceptible to demonic attack.

The old covenant prophets describe God as a ferocious lion in several other places. Yet when the Light dawned and God fully revealed Himself in Christ, a different picture was painted. John the apostle was given a heavenly revelation of this when he beheld the Lion of the tribe of Judah. When he turned his gaze towards this Lion, he did not see a ferocious beast. Instead, he saw "a Lamb standing, as if slain" (see Rev. 5:5-6). The full face of God was revealed as one of mercy and grace. One who did not retaliate even when men spit into His face and struck nails into His Son's hands. Instead, He was revealed as the One who spread out His arms and cried out for forgiveness and healing. His lion-like fierceness and power is revealed as being that of conquering love and of a relentless pursuit of His children. All along, God was coming as a Savior and a Protector—even though for a season of time under the law there would be an incomplete picture of His true nature and being. This would be under the "shadow" of the law (see Heb. 10:1).

The apostle John was told that the Lion of Judah (the One revealed as a slain Lamb) had "overcome" (Rev. 5:5). What was Jesus overcoming? He was destroying the curse that came upon mankind through unrighteousness. He did this by giving us His own righteousness instead. The accuser had raged over man and utilized the law of sin and death in order to steal, kill, and destroy—and this was part of the "wrath" that the law inflicted. The powers and authorities of heaven were armed with firm weaponry and demanded their right to inflict war, murder, rape, theft, plague, and famine according to the curse of the law.

When God showed up on planet earth as Jesus, He was the One who healed the infirmities that Satan caused (see Luke 13:16). He was the One who raised up those who fell into death. He was the One who brought joy where there was sorrow and food where there was hunger. In His physical life, Jesus came against every penalty of the law—and all of it pointed to the final reversal of the curse in His own resurrection.

The book of Colossians explains this concept further. It is a wonderful New Testament companion to the truths laid out allegorically in the Song of Solomon. In Colossians, Paul not only refs to us being complete in Christ and having no more blemishes, but he also says that we are *free from accusation*. He later goes on to say that, through the cross, God cancelled the written code of the law that stood against us and was hostile towards us. That hostility was like a lion or a leopard lying in wait to destroy the people of God because of their transgressions. So Christ came to take away this hostility by nailing it to the cross. He took the full curse on Himself. Look at how Paul explains more of what was going on behind this "hostility"...

*When you were dead in your transgressions and the uncircumcision of your flesh, He made you alive together with Him, having forgiven us **all our transgressions**, having **canceled out** the certificate of debt consisting of decrees against us, which was **hostile to us;** and He has taken it out of the way, having nailed it to the cross. When He had **disarmed the rulers and authorities**, He made a public display of them, having triumphed over them through Him.*
(Col. 2:13-15)

The entirety of the wrath of the law fell on the physical body of Christ when He absorbed it completely into Himself. As a result, He "disarmed" the powers and authorities and "triumphed" over them. The powers and authorities are the demonic forces that used the transgression of the law to inflict death and destruction on humanity. There was certainly anger and wrath within God, but this wrath was directed at sin itself, because sin hinders our love, freedom and blessing. When man chose to live in a false and sinful identity (and also chose to live outside the protection of the law before Christ), they would incur that wrath on themselves. Nonetheless, it was never God's intention or desire to see people suffer these things. He takes no pleasure in the death of the wicked. God has always loved the sinner himself, and has always remembered His image and likeness still resident within man. Jesus came to completely forgive us of our transgressions and called us to awaken to the true love of God and our true identity in Him. In the process, He also took away the enemy's main weapon—the accusation of the law through sin.

The wonderful thing about grace is that the law's curses are completely taken away and the enemy has no more legal right to attack us, because we are completely righteous in Christ. This is not based upon our own obedience, but upon the obedience of Christ. Because of this, the lions and leopards have no more place to "lie in wait" in order to pounce on us. However, the enemy does not want us to know this. He wants us to go back to the law and trust in our own abilities to attain righteousness in order to reap blessing and protection. He does not want us to know that the law was fulfilled and there is no more wrath and penalty against us.

Unfortunately, when we continue to live in fear of wrath and judgment, we empower the devil and his demonic host through their deception, not knowing that their authority to attack and accuse has been completely stripped away at the cross. We are now the ones with authority over them. At the summit of Truth they are already under our feet, for we are united with Christ who is seated in righteousness at the right hand of the Father.

An awakening to this element of grace will bring the church to a whole new level of consistent and steady victory. This is why a pure conscience, rooted in Christ's finished work, is perhaps our greatest weapon against darkness. In fact, when Paul discusses the full armor of God in Ephesians, he begins with the belt of *amana*—truth. This is because the belt in Roman armor was the binding piece by which all of the other equipment stayed connected and firm. To lose the truth of our innocence in God's eyes, and the love He has always had towards us, is to lose sight of everything else. The toothless lion can then paralyze us with fear and the spotted leopard will make us doubt who we are. We can then be unlawfully devoured as a result.

Yet by the word of our testimony at Calvary and the shed blood of the Lamb (and by holding to this Word, even in the face of extreme persecution), we easily and swiftly overcome demonic wrath. The law has been fulfilled in Christ and all the fiery arrows it pointed against us in accusation are now quenched in the waters of Christ's baptism into death. Christ is the Lion of the tribe of Judah who has overcome the curse, even though a false lion still roams the land and tries to sound like God by using the law against us.

So in other words, the redeemed Bride is being called to come away from the old paradigm of wrath and judgment, and from the fears attached to it. She is to no longer live under a dark cloud of worry over whether or not she is obeying the law enough to keep away the curse and the devourer. Such was the paradigm under the old covenant, but not even a hint of that thinking is allowed in the new. Remember that "the fig tree has ripened its figs" and the old covenant is now fulfilled and thus obsolete. We can now rest in the obedience of Christ instead of striving to be obedient enough to somehow keep away the lions and leopards of this world. Jesus obeyed the law on our behalf and freely bestowed upon us the complete benefits of His own righteousness (which means complete blessing—not a single curse). Now, in the words of Paul, we are "saved from wrath" (Rom. 5:9).

Shadow and Fear

All of this gives us a deeper understanding into the Shulammite's worries over the "shadows" around her. Remember that she was waiting for the day when all the shadows would flee away and a new day would dawn. She was waiting for the final day when no lie or demonic influence would be present. Now the metaphor of a shadow is incredibly powerful here. Shadows contain no true substance or form. It is only the result of something blocking the light and thus causing an absence of illumination.

So even though you may see the enemy's activity, it is has no true substance and validity. There is no true form. So many people empower the devil and his host through their fear of him. They believe he still has a "form" of strength and authority, but he is really empty and weak. His only power consists in lies and accusations, and when we give into these things we only empower a false identity and reap a curse that no longer needs to be there. Then this liar gets us to think that God is the one putting the curse on us!

How many people go through life and when bad things happen they believe that God is punishing them? How desperately the world needs to hear the Song of the Gospel... God is for us! He is no longer counting men's sins against them (see 2 Cor. 5:14-21...really, go look at it again). We ourselves need to awaken to this truth and then go out and awaken others to it as well.

We even need to go and awaken whole nations to this reality of grace. There are sadly many people who speak from an old covenant perspective and believe that God Himself is dumping His wrath and anger onto sinful countries. They believe the Lord God is inciting warlords to rape and kill women and then take their kids into rebel armies. They believe the Spirit of Holiness is reaching His hand down from heaven and shifting tectonic plates so that whole families can fall into a pit, hit their heads on jagged rocks and die from suffocation and bleeding. They believe that God the Father is making orphans out of disasters and ripping families apart. They believe Jesus is behind a 767 cockpit flying into buildings.

But none of this is the work of the Father of Lights. If you want to see His judgment in action, you can look no further than the cross. It was there that He took the full consequences of sin onto Himself. He hung from the tower of the cross, allowing our hatred to fly into Him instead of the other way around. The Lion was revealed as a Lamb and His roar was one of mercy—mercy that *completely* triumphed over judgment.

The enemy now has no more right to inflict the curse onto mankind. It is the rising Shulammite church who should be the first to stand firm in this reality. Then, as ministers of reconciliation, the church is to go out and release this Gospel of victory to all mankind. What an amazing journey and destiny the Lord has in store for His awakened Bride!

The Purpose of Everything Said Thus Far...

As I write this book I'm aware that some may say that I've made too big of a deal of issues like law, religiosity, and the theology of Christ's finished work—that I am not focusing enough on the journey of love and intimacy that this Song communicates. I appreciate this potential concern, but let me say that the primary thing that hinders intimacy with God is fear, law and condemnation.

Now intimacy and love is certainly what it is all about. The apostle Paul said, "the *goal* of our instruction is love." Nonetheless, the instruction itself, which leads to love, is a teaching that involves the breakdown of the wall, the bed, and the lions and leopards. Love, he explains, comes "from a pure heart, a good conscience, and a sincere faith" (1 Tim. 1:5). When our conscience is washed in the blood of the Lamb, when our faith is rooted in His work on the cross, and when we realize our spotted hearts have been made new, then true and lasting love is easily attained. Intimacy becomes something with which you don't need a book to help you. It is the simple fruit of being awakened to your identity and to the love revealed on Calvary.

So the goal and purpose is always intimacy and relationship. That is the end of everything spoken thus far. Every true revelation from heaven is meant to lead to a fruitful life of love. In the second half of Solomon's Song we will explore this more deeply. For now, we must realize that love and intimacy cannot be conjured up or created. As we said before, fruit is organic, not manmade. It grows naturally on the vine. We are the branches that are meant to *rest* in the vine of Christ's love. So for this reason we have had to deal with the suffocating lies that come against the flow of these truths in the Shulammite's life.

In summary, Jesus is acknowledging the lions and leopards of the law and of accusation. The Shulammite is to move right past them, for she has been given a higher perspective of grace. The shadows of the law and the lies of the enemy have no more power over her and should no longer hinder the flow of Christ's heavenly life through her earthly branch (Jn. 15:5). We may empower the devil through our fear of him and our doctrines about demons and all their authority, but in the highest perspective of heaven, they have been completely defeated. The flow of grace can only be quenched through fear, through clinging to a false identity, and through remaining under the lie of a false separation from God.

But love, intimacy and fruitfulness—a land of milk and honey—is set before us like a rich banqueting table. The Kingdom of God is "at hand." This means it is *within reach*. The Shulammite can easily taste it if she would only let go of the religion that burnt her in the vineyards of her brothers and the voice of the accuser that still tries to whisper in her ear. But this taste and victory comes through the perspective of *Amana*. It begins by seeing the fullness of the land, trusting in His Word, and receiving His love. The wall of the law is taken down and there is no more wrath upon her. She is now her Beloved's. No shadow or false lion can stand in the way of that truth.

I pray the Lord reveals this same thing to your heart, especially as we conclude our present journey.

21 The Highest View

You have ravished my heart, my sister, my bride
You have ravished my heart with one glance of your eyes
With one bead of your necklace
(4:9 NKJV)

A young child could sit down with a piece of paper containing only one sentence—the ninth verse of the fourth chapter of the Song of Solomon—and he could begin to study and meditate on the words within that verse. He might decide to give himself to a lifetime of prayer in seeking to understand the depths of this one line. He could research every commentary on the Song and talk about it with every known authority on the text—Jewish and Christian. Going from secondary school to a college education geared towards understanding and grasping these same words, he might then pursue a life career built around the same thing. And he could live a long and satisfying life as he continued this one pursuit. In his retirement, he could sit down once more with that same piece of paper and continue to read, and pray, and ponder.

And in his passage to eternity, he could continue this pondering and begin to inquire of angels as to its beauty and truth. He could find great men and women who had passed long before him and discuss it with them as well. The long flood of his life and now the beginning of his enjoyment of eternity would pass into ageless memories. From one eon of eternity to the next, he could continue this same pursuit. He could persist in setting his focus on that piece of paper and that single verse written therein. This person, who was once a boy, then a man, then a grandfather, then a spirit who passed into timelessness, could move into new epochs of eternity and new realms of infinite space, continuing to study this one single verse all along the way.

And in doing all of this, he may discover only a fragment of its depth and meaning...

At the peak of the revelation given so far, and hidden within the depths of this one crowning verse, we find the Lord becoming completely transparent—vulnerable even, if we could use that word. This is an intimate and in-depth look into the heart of our Maker, the very Creator of heaven and earth. I can think of only two other times that this vulnerability in God was revealed. One was when He became a frail human baby and allowed Himself to be cared for by human parents. The other time was when He hung naked on a cross and spread out His arms in love. Remarkably, these acts—both becoming a man and dying as one—flowed from the deep love and passion that we find expressed in this Song and especially in this one verse.

As an aside, this may be part of the reason as to why the message of the Song of Songs has often been hidden under the guise of marriage wisdom or seen as just an old drama depicting an ancient king's marriage. Perhaps this is why only a relatively small amount of saints and mystics over the centuries have really plumbed the depths of this book from the perspective of union between Christ and His beloved church. The Lord does not throw His pearls before swine, and some of the most precious pearls of His Word are hidden in the fourth chapter of the Song of Solomon.

Yet even though it is a hidden mystery, this is a season of time when the mysteries of heaven are being unveiled at an accelerating rate. As Daniel prophesied, "knowledge would increase" in the latter days (see Dan.12:4). This is not only in reference to human knowledge, but also to spiritual knowledge. And true spiritual knowledge is not just some ethereal insight into the nature of the universe or the spirit realm. At its peak and height, spiritual knowledge comes from looking into the eyes of God and seeing His face and knowing His heart. Such are the ultimate mysteries of heaven being revealed to the saints in this hour.

So what is the unsearchable message found in this one verse? What is this transcendent, intimate "pearl" that I am referring to? Part of it is the open and honest declaration by God that we *do something* real and powerful to His heart. We "ravish" it, the King says—with only one glance of our eyes...

In order to get somewhat of a grasp on this verse, we will need to look at this word "ravish" and explore some other translations of the text. My hope is that nobody would leave this chapter or this book without getting a clear picture of what is really being communicated by God. It is easy to water down His words in fear of something sounding blasphemous or even too good to be true. So we're going to remove all the religious water and attempt to drink down this verse pure and straight.

The Ravished Heart of God

The word "ravish" literally means to overwhelm, enrapture, stun, or transport into another place. When the Lord looks at us... Actually, let me do the difficult job of writing and speaking beyond any walls of resistance in your own heart and make this even more personal... When the Lord looks at *you*, His heart is overcome by something that we can only compare to the human experience of being overwhelmed and carried away. For those who have held a child in their arms and looked at their innocence and frailty in love, you may be able to taste what I am referring to here. Or to someone who has held a lover in his or her arms, an intimate friend and spouse, and looked into their eyes in a moment of clarity and gratitude, you too may have some understanding as well. But even these transcendent moments are only glimpses of what we find happening in the Lord when He looks at us.

There are times when the heart is overrun and taken possession by something outside of itself, leaving us immobilized in ecstasy and awe. Sometimes this comes when you are caught off-guard by an awe-inspiring view of nature or when your eyes meet someone of stunning physical beauty. Like it or not, this is all part of what the Hebrew word for "ravished" entails. This is what has happened in the heart of God when He looks at you as His child and friend. The New American Standard Bible says that His heart actually starts *beating faster* when He looks at us. There is a real reaction in God that He cannot contain and so it must spill out.

Another way to translate this verse is by saying, "You have conquered My heart!" The New International Version says that we have "stolen" His heart! The very center and wellspring of God's life, His eternal heart, has been possessed by an unrelenting love for us. For all eternity we will hold a place of unique privilege and joy within Him. This ravished heart is probably what inspired God to press through the pain of human history and the shame of the cross in order to possess us as His own—and to see His own glory fully manifested in our lives. Another translation actually says that with one glance of our eyes we give the Lord "courage" (Sng. 4:9 AMP). We actually enliven the heart of God and move Him into passionate action. This is a love that is real, relational and uncontrollably fierce. There is no place for insecurity or fear in the light of such fiery love. If we truly knew this, insecurity and discouragement would be as foreign to us as the far side of space.

I hope you are starting to get somewhat of a picture here. This chapter is only a meant to be postcard. It is not the real view. In order to see the view yourself, you must go beyond the words and allow the Holy Spirit to bring you personally into the place of truth. But hopefully the postcard is clear enough to let you know the trip is well worth it. Thankfully, it is God's pleasure and delight to reveal these things to those who ask. There is no need for begging God to give you insight into these things, for He wants to give it to you more than you even want it. Only believe and rest in the confidence that He desires for you to know His love more than anything else. Then watch as He leads you in every area of your life to take hold of these truths. I promise, it'll take about a million years before you've exhausted even a fraction of its magnitude and depth.

The Spark of the Song

I really wanted to explore this verse at a deeper level because it provides the impetus and spark for everything said thus far. Throughout this Song, the Lord has spoken amazing words of love and truth to His Bride. If we're not careful, however, we can rationally take these words as plain "biblical truth" without understanding the context of their origin and meaning. We must come to recognize that these words (and really all of His Word to us) do not come from some dry and boring entity who speaks with a stoic, booming voice on a throne. It does not come from some big Zeus-like god sitting on a white chair and declaring that he loves the world as though he's some monstrous robot who is programmed to say such things just because it's in his nature to do so.

No. These words come from a perfect, unchanging, and yet relational and spontaneous Being who is moved by things—like we are moved by earthly love and beauty. They come from a place of infinite, passionate, and "ravished" love. Such is the reason for every verse we've covered and the drive behind Jesus's eternal plan of redemption.

Such discussions on the Personhood of God have the potential to conflict with our nice and neat, western, theological "God-boxes." We have our systematic lists and breakdowns of the nature of God (as though man could somehow describe and systematize the Eternal), and this feels a whole lot safer to us. I'm referring to the nice God-boxes where we use certain words like "omnipotent, omniscient, omnipresent, etc...." Now these things are all true. However, I would also add that there is a wildness and spontaneity in God from which mankind finds their own ability to emote and act spontaneously and passionately.

Man has had the tendency to imagine God as this impersonal controlled force sitting on a throne in the center of the universe. But there is a Person on that throne who has a soul with traits that humans know of as emotion, passion, depth, and personality. Many prefer to follow a religious system with clear to-do lists and a corresponding religious textbook in place of this reality. But sooner or later we will all be confronted with the wildness and personal-ness of God.

The Lord is certainly holy and *other* and beyond our comprehension. This is important to recognize as well. But we have most likely heard that in many other places. For now, let us see how real and close and passionate the Lord is. God did not come to us as a bright beam of light circling around the fields of Israel, nor did He come as some white-bearded sage sitting on a mountain in a lotus position. He came to us as a carpenter and as a friend. Then He went on to save the world not by conjuring up some magical potion or by using brute force, but by giving up His life and fully opening His heart to us.

From the Same Origin

In this particular verse, the Lord addresses the Shulammite as "His sister." It is the first time He calls us His sister as well as His bride. This shows us that our identity and relationship with Jesus goes beyond the consistent marriage analogy of the text. We are also His siblings, which speaks to the fact that we were born from the same divine seed, and are a part of the same heavenly family. Of course, Jesus is our origin and has always existed—He is not created, but eternal. Yet there is a mystery here showing that we are "of the Father" in similar fashion to Christ. We were birthed from the very Trinity and now we are joined into Their circle as "partakers of the divine nature" (2 Pet. 1:4). Jesus is the Son of God and the church is God's daughter, Christ's sister. You could also say that we are the sons of God—but the point is that we have a divine origin. "You are gods," Jesus affirmed, when He quoted the 82nd Psalm (see Jn. 10:34).

It is at this point that we are treading onto blasphemous territory. But before you think that I'm getting too carried away with this and perhaps exalting humanity too much, let me emphasize and make clear that in this Song Jesus is seeing the physical image and likeness of Yahweh in His sister and bride. She, and all of Adam's children, were created as earthly reflections of the Eternal One. It is why angels minister to us and why heaven and earth responds to us—whether positively or negatively. It is the image of God's glory within us that is causing Jesus's overwhelming declarations.

Yet this is not a disclaimer to water down what has already been said. Bearing "His image and likeness" is not some aloof concept that is separate from who we are intrinsically—as though there is the "image-bearing" side of us, then there is little old sinful "me" over here (and in order to be humble I have to acknowledge that little-old-sinful-me and not get too carried away by the image-bearing side). No! This is who we are, through and through. We are the pearl of great price for which Jesus died. We are the joy set before Him and the reason why He endured the shame of the cross. Sin was only a deception and marring of this original glory and innocence.

God has placed His very glory in us and He sees this glory from His perfect perspective. This is the reason that His heart is so ravished, because He is seeing His own infinite beauty reflected in another. Now it's important to know that we are not just impersonal mirrors for God to look into so that He can stare at Himself all day. We are *personal* mirrors that carry our own uniqueness. A uniqueness that still flows from His overall being. We are just as much *other* as we are one. Hence, the marriage analogy all throughout the Song is still a great representation of this relationship, since it speaks of two becoming one. Even in complete union, there is still a place for distinction and relationship.

Obviously, all of these realities concerning our identity are "of God and not from ourselves" (2 Cor. 4:7). This unsurpassable value is hidden in the clay vessel of our human body. But all of that simply means that we did nothing to achieve or earn this glory and beauty. We can take no credit for it. And yet we can still own it, enjoy it, and fully identify with it—with thanksgiving and praise unto God alone.

Jesus looks at His Bride and He sees one who is equally yoked with Himself. She is the express image and likeness of God just as He is—only He is the Redeemer and Source and Initiator of that likeness. This God has done the unthinkable and perhaps what every being in heaven thought impossible—He has created another being who would perfectly reflect Himself. Though the Shulammite is often held back by fear and religion, this is who she is, and all along He has intensely desired that she would know these things as well.

Now with all of that being said, it is very important to note that "one bead" of her necklace causes this powerful reaction in the heart of God. In the first chapter of the Song, we discussed how the necklace describes that which outwardly adorns our lives. It is the fruit of the Spirit coming forth in the life of a believer. It is His glory radiating outwardly for all to see. This then is an incredibly encouraging statement, because it is not even the whole complete necklace that causes this reaction in the Lord. Just one strand, one pearl of outer adornment, causes this rapture and joy in His heart! In other words, even in the believer who may be showing only one outward sign of the life of God in them—*they also ravish, conquer, and enliven the very soul of their Maker.*

This is because our beauty goes beyond what we can see in our outward lives. That isn't meant to downplay the importance of the outward manifestations of the Spirit. We have already covered this element of grace. The outward adornment of God's nature, like jewelry on the body, comes forth as we simply awaken to the truth of who we are—apart from our own efforts and abilities. The fact of the matter is that we are already stunning and beautiful in the eyes of God. This alone brings rest to the soul. And in time, we will all see what God has seen all along. His glory will outwardly adorn our lives. And so we will *know* as we have always been known (see 1 Cor. 13:12).

True Clarity

We have been following the Shulammite along a trail filled with strange and simple things. We have seen a seat covered in mercy and blood. A tree casting a protective shadow. A table filled with the most delightful and delicious foods. Myrrh and incense and fragrant life. Vineyards and wine. These things have all communicated something that the entire world is searching after. People have many different words to describe this search. Everyone has different opinions as to what they believe is at the pinnacle of reality—whether it's nirvana, paradise, enlightenment, or the third heaven. But the Song of the Ages has made it quite simple and clear.

At the summit of all Truth, a pure view has finally emerged. Clouds often obscure it, emotions and circumstances can get in the way, and the humidity of deception can cast a silky haze over the horizon of our perspective. But in a moment of clarity, at the height of the message found through Christ's cross, we see the full picture. God has completely opened Himself up to the searching Shulammite and has revealed the overwhelming love within His heart.

At the height of all Truth, the peak of all that is truly real and eternal, is a God who is passionately in love with us—and with Whom we share an eternal and sacred union. This is the summit of everything. Furthermore, this union and love are not dependent upon anything we can do or earn. These things do not wax and wane like the moon from an earthly perspective. Instead, they are like the moon from a heavenly viewpoint, which steadily orbits the planet in faithfulness and grace. God's unfailing love and His covenant of peace forever encircle our lives even when the passing shadows of life appear to obscure it.

Those shadows, as well as the lions, leopards and walls, have been built up and reinforced ever since our departure from Eden. For countless amounts of people, these walls are all they have ever known. They may have tasted slight bits of His fruit and have even seen slivers of light pass through the cracks of their fears and religious dogmas. But few have believed they could come away from their wall and fully embrace the lyrics of God's Song. Yet these things are changing. Great encouragement has come to the church from the heart of God. He is dead-set on tearing down our walls and lifting us up out of the bed of fear and deception. Nothing can stop the tide that is coming in to His people, when all will finally see the glory of His Truth.

The kisses of His Word and Spirit have come in full force, just as the Shulammite originally asked. In this one verse, we have found the words that form this kiss, words that go beyond the heart and imagination's capacity to understand. And perhaps this is a good time to remind ourselves that we should not even attempt to lean on our own understanding. Sometimes trusting and leaning into the wildness of God's Word is all that we can do. Indeed, a kiss is not something you are meant to logically understand and analyze. You simply lean into it and receive it.

This is our highest joy—the reality of divine love and of union with Christ. It is from this place of Truth that we will journey forward with the Shulammite towards a fruitful life of love. As the church comes into this place, Eden shall blossom again in the hearts of God's people. The flowers of our divine life and origin shall come forth in full fragrance and peace. And as this blossoming begins in a hidden way within our hearts, the flowers of our lives will soon drop seeds upon the dry soil of this planet. Before long, fruit will appear all around us. The wilderness shall be turned into an oasis and rivers shall flow again on the barren heights. High places will be made low and valleys will be raised up. The world will change.

And all will see the glory of the Lord revealed in His awakened Temple and Bride.

Third Selah

I always appreciate the moments of "Selah" and reflection that Solomon's father David wove into his own songs. You might imagine young Solomon gleaning from his dad as he watched him compose great works of worship and adoration. But what David began, Solomon would finish. David wrote the plans of the temple, but Solomon would turn them into reality (see 1 Chr. 28:11). David wrote songs of love and worship in the Psalms—but Solomon would bring these melodies to perfection in his own Song that speaks of the Lamb and His Bride.

So let's take one more moment to utilize David's *Selah* in his son's eternal Song. It does our soul so well to pause, reflect and just bask in the shade of the words that have gone before us. We might think of Joshua, who was asked to meditate on the Word day and night after being told to "come away" and enter into the Promised Land (see Josh. 1). We are already in the Promise of union with Christ, but our life manifests this reality as our hearts chew down and swallow the beauty of His Word. Now many might have a hard time swallowing some of the things that have been revealed so far. So you might need to especially meditate on the fact that *your teeth are as newly shorn sheep, washed and bearing twins.* You have the ability to spiritually understand the Truth, even if your mind can't wrap itself around it. The Spirit of understanding is resident within you. Do not be anxious that these great lyrics and messages of God's love are beyond your ability to enjoy.

The preceding words of the Song have come hidden in a parable like Jesus's words often came to people when He walked the earth. But they are nonetheless there for us to discover as we look into His eyes and behold the depths of His love—which led to His very death on a cross. His cross is indeed the wooden instrument upon which this Song is played.

Meanwhile, David and all the house of Israel were celebrating
before the LORD with all kinds of instruments made of fir wood...
(2 Sam. 6:5)

In the next verses of the Song, the Lord is going to continue in His adoration and exaltation of the Bride as He calls her away. And unfortunately, we will uncover one more period of pain and isolation as the depths of religious branding come out in full blast. But now is not the time to look into those things. Now is the time to rest on the summit of Truth, to behold its view of the Promise, and to allow our hearts to open a little wider to the greatest and sweetest melody of all.

The Song of the Ages infinitely plays on. It will continue playing whether you are awake or asleep. Its lyrics will continue to pour forth whether you are lost in worship or in a fog of doubt. Whether you are deep in prayer or deep in the darkness of self-lies, it will still continue its sweet hum. Even when you hurt yourself or others, this Song plays on from the heights of heaven. And when you are awake to its beauty and treating yourself and others accordingly, the Song plays all the more clearer.

Aware or unaware, this Song is true. There is no work to somehow make all of this a reality. It already is—and our hearts are simply called to tune in.

To be continued...

About the Author

Nick Padovani is a husband, a father, a social worker, and a friend of Jesus. He is also the pastor of a beautiful and flourishing church in northern New Jersey. It is his joy and passion to see God's children awaken to their full inheritance in the love of Christ.

Find more of his writings and teachings
as well as general updates at:
nickpadovani.wordpress.com

CPSIA information can be obtained
at www.ICGtesting.com
Printed in the USA
BVHW041122170423
662477BV00001B/55

9 781498 430357